The Other Man
The Other Woman

The Other Man The Other Woman

Understanding and Coping
with Extramarital Affairs

by Joel D. Block, Ph.D.

GROSSET & DUNLAP
A FILMWAYS COMPANY
Publishers • New York

The publishers gratefully acknowledge permission to reprint material from the following:

I Can If I Want To by Arnold Lazarus and Allen Fay. Copyright © 1975 by Arnold A. Lazarus and Allen Fay. Used by permission of William Morrow and Company, Inc.

The Intimate Enemy by George R. Bach and Peter Wyden. Copyright © 1968, 1969 by George R. Bach and Peter Wyden. Used by permission of William Morrow and Company, Inc.

The Affair by Morton Hunt. Copyright © 1969 by Morton Hunt. Used by permission of World Publishing Company.

To my intramarital loves,
Gail, Abbey, Fred

Contents

Acknowledgments

With all my thanks and affection to:

The men and women who shared a segment of their personal lives with me.

My teachers at the State University of New York in Oswego, at Syracuse University, and during my postdoctoral studies. Although they did not contribute directly to this work, I would not have had the courage to consider it without their cherished influence.

My mother, Rose Block, for caring enough to get me moving many years ago when I needed a push and for encouraging me when I needed praise.

Gail Block, my wife, who by appreciating my peculiar psyche, helps make life more fun-filled and productive.

Introduction

We humans are very complex. We want change, but we dislike disruption; we like the new, but we cherish the old; we desire thrill and excitement, but we put a premium on security; ambiguity seems interesting, but too much of it provokes anxiety; we may seek familiarity, but when we find it we become bored. This ambivalence is present in all aspects of our lives, but in affairs of the heart, it is more acute.

To fit our multifaceted emotional beings into the confines of the marital arrangement is not easy. As a means of attaining fulfillment for two individuals, the institution of marriage has limitations and imperfections. A working marriage—one that provides mutual pleasure— requires frequent repair and readjustment. Many marriages don't work—or they don't work for long. Stage, television, movies, and real life present us with frequent examples of marital strife. The divorce rate in our country is very high. Yet the marital relationship offers something significant to many people, for the great majority of those who divorce remarry. Marriage is not disappearing. The institution is alive, if not thriving.

Most of us know that even at its best marriage cannot meet all the needs of both spouses all the time. Marital lives are not conducted in isolation; husbands and wives are in contact with numerous other people every day. As a matter of course, they will experience satisfactions from these encounters. Many spouses are not only *not* disturbed that "outsiders" serve in this capacity, but also relieved that they themselves are not obligated to meet each and every need or whim of their mates.

But what if that need or whim is sexual? Faithfulness being ordinarily seen as faithfulness in the flesh, sexual transgressions have always been highly disturbing. The momentousness of sex —though exaggerated by our culture—produces emotional turmoil. Temptation creates more of a conflict in the sexual area than in any other area of life simply because we value sex so highly today. Sex is in.

Attraction to people other than one's mate is also in. Actually, it always has been—the mere fact that there are men and women establishes attraction as a constant. However, when the average life span was between twenty-five and thirty-five years, and when married couples and their families lived and worked in small self-sufficient units, the opportunities for realizing one's desires for emotional/sexual involvement outside marriage were severely limited. Our ancestors were confined not only by stricter views of the obligations of wedlock but also by the technological restrictions of their time. Now, with urbanization, larger communities, greatly improved mobility, and eased social restraints on sexual behavior, extramarital sex is not only more tempting but far more realizable.

As a psychologist and marital therapist, I have become sensitive to individual differences and understand that some people are more attracted to the extramarital experience, but the temptation is a universal one. In a world so impersonal, so disconnected, so unconcerned about the individual's needs, many of us find that marriage provides only part of what we hunger for. If that hunger turns to lust—the sexual and psychological excitement of a new person—the ground rules forbid us to go further than fantasy. But human nature is not rebuffed by the restriction; rules beg to be broken. Reliable sociological evidence reveals that affairs, from the one-night stand to the grand amour, are increasing in prevalence.

Whether or not we approve of the rising incidence of extramarital liaisons, we cannot reasonably deny that this is a subject of considerable interest to nearly all adults. Yet there is surprisingly little nonfiction writing about it. There are a few statistical studies, brief case histories by therapists, a sprinkling of books, and enormous numbers of admonitions written by the clergy. Only in the form of fiction (not always a reliable guide to reality), is there a deluge of material.

A book on extramarital sex that bridges the gap between imagination (the novel) and numbers (the statistical study) is rare. One that offers a guideline for understanding and coping with what is to many people a dilemma seems to be nonexistent. Just as we have, until recently, ignored the fact of death, so have we overlooked the psychology of sexual partnership outside marriage. This book will, I hope, partly fill this gap. It is not a scientific, statistical study nor is it intended to replace therapy. It is not a prescription for or a proscription against extramarital sex. My purpose has not been to condemn or condone; it has been to produce an honest guide to the risks, consequences, emotional joys, traumas, and traps generated by the institution of marriage and one of its more enticing complications—the extramarital affair.

Author's Note

Every significant emotion and deed described in this book is drawn from real life. Some of the people have been in therapy with me; many have not. Occasionally, several people's stories were combined to illustrate an issue, but the integrity of the psychological dynamics has been protected. Naturally, every effort has been made to assure anonymity. Names, various physical characteristics, and circumstantial descriptions have been altered to make identification of a particular person impossible.

Desire and Prevalence

A Sampler

Kay, a forty-six-year-old medical social worker who had never before been separated from her husband of seventeen years, was seated at a professional convention next to Donald, a physician in his early forties. They got to talking; she found him immensely charming and intelligent, and eventually the subject turned to sex. Halfway through the night they became lovers. She spent three carefree, flirtatious days with him; then the convention ended and they went their separate ways to homes only sixty miles apart.

Kay, for her part, reacted to the experience rather dramatically:

"My outlook on life was completely changed. The affair made me aware of my frustrated need to think and to communicate with someone I felt tuned in to. Before, I had been asleep; I had been living with a sense of incompleteness without knowing it. It was a painful realization; and one that led me to end my marriage. Yet I do not regret what happened. I would rather be aware—know what I want and not have it—than to live out my life without ever having known. But it's been difficult. There was a time when I looked forward to my future with my husband; it was a comforting, secure thought, growing old together. Now those images are agonizing. He has been hurt. I try not to think of him."

The experience also had an impact on Donald, though a substantially lesser one:

"Kay was the first real affair I had since I got married. I had gone to bed with two other women before her, but they were quickies. I felt guilty about them, and as a result, I lavished more affection on my wife, Janet.

"I was restless and dissatisfied with my marriage, but I had no desire to get out of it. Several women at the hospital were becoming increasingly attractive to me; secretly I was hungering for a woman to grab me and seduce me. I'm not a passive man, but I felt so obligated to Janet that I thought it would be necessary for another woman to be very aggressive. That was all fantasy. When I met Kay, I practically accosted her. I didn't let up until we made love. The last night of the convention we spent together was the closest I had felt to anybody in a decade."

Kay and Donald maintained contact over the next year. He would occasionally ask her to spend time with him; sometimes a few days, sometimes just an afternoon. She was now divorced and he was still married. In between visits, she went out with other men and he had begun to see other women; though they grew closer and considered themselves in love, neither spoke of an exclusive commitment. Kay was convinced, instead, that fairly soon their affair was going to end. The way she saw it, she had two choices. One was to find someone else who was available for marriage; the other was to continue in the present relationship as long as it lasted. She was leaning toward the latter. Kay spoke of her arrangement in a quiet firm voice:

"I couldn't get myself to ask Don to leave his wife for my sake. He'd been pressured all his adult life by his wife; I wouldn't allow myself to become an additional pressure. Besides, it would backfire. His wife had driven him out with her nagging; he started staying away from home more and more to avoid her whining and I was determined not to be categorized with her.

"Anyway, his wife wasn't my competition; she was a non person to me. Don went places without her whenever he could. She didn't care, so long as she was given enough money for her expensive tastes. A couple of times a week he spends the night at his office where there is an attached apartment, he tells his wife he has too much to do to come home. That's where I go to be with him; he prefers not to stay over at my house. With my children nearly grown, I feel able to move into his place for a couple of days at a time, but usually he becomes restless and finds some way to suggest it's time for him to get back home. He says it's for appearance's sake, but I don't believe that; it's because he wants to be alone—or, more likely, because he wants to play around with other women. I hate that part, but what can I do? I just can't get myself to discuss it with him."

*

Larry is a fairly typical banker, specializing in real estate, who comfortably maintaines a suburban country club lifestyle. He was born and raised in an upper-middle-class WASP family and married an almost ideal WASP woman with whom he has lived contentedly for the past nine years. They have three well-adjusted children. He is not really unhappy about the life he leads; he is quite satisfied with his present income and he makes a point of not joining in the heavy drinking and womanizing at banking conventions.

On occasion, Larry travels to nearby cities for several days at a time in connection with his work. He accepts these trips as part of his responsibility but certainly does not regard them as the highlight of his job. One such trip that he had anticipated with some apprehension turned out to be much more productive than he had imagined. At the conclusion of the day's business, he arranged to finish up the next day, one day earlier than expected. He was pleasantly surprised and quite relieved. On the way out, he met his business contact's secretary, Muriel, and was struck by her appearance; she was small and slender, almost childlike, with black shiny hair in an Afro. Her face was long and her eyes, though hidden by excessive makeup were bright. She was, at most, in her late twenties.

"Just before I left the office, I did something impulsive and very odd for me. I asked Muriel out to dinner. Surprised and a bit apprehensive, she accepted. At dinner, I found her to be a hell of a good conversationalist—quick, incisive, and unafraid to express her opinions. Refreshing. When she spoke, she looked even prettier. There was something about her warmth and personality that attracted me. It was as if I were a very, very impressive person. After dinner, I dropped her off at her apartment but I couldn't get her out of my thoughts. In the morning, I felt a definite excitement as I called to arrange the next day's business and the next evening's dinner with Muriel. I questioned this: 'I'm a married man, I'm happy, what the hell am I doing?' But all I could think of was being with Muriel. It was crazy—I felt like a teenager again. I learned that there were a number of men in her life, but I didn't care. She was good company and I enjoyed talking with her; that was enough. But was it? Back home thoughts of her kept intruding while I was at the bank or in the house playing with the children. I found myself looking forward to rather than dreading my trips to that city. In her company, I felt light, playful—something I'd never really experienced before. I was brought up to be staid, emotionless, and compulsively achievement-oriented. Muriel was easygoing; she had a devil-may-care attitude that was infectious. One evening, she kissed me good night. Up to this point, there had been nothing more than innocent hand holding. I wasn't really ready for more. Just breaking my usual 100 percent business and efficiency routine was monumental for me. The thought of getting involved was overwhelming."

After he had known Muriel for about eight months, Larry began to have a change of heart. The lack of sexual intimacy started to bother him. It was like an unfinished project. Not that things were bad at home. He was having regular and satisfactory sexual relations; there was a mutual warm interchange between himself and his wife. Nor did he find Muriel all that attractive. Yet the longer he continued to see her, the more he became obsessed with "making his move." On the one hand, he feared that an overt, bold approach might offend her, but on the other hand, he felt compelled to break the brother-sister pattern.

"I was considering all this when one stormy February night Muriel turned to me and suggested we take a suite at the Plaza. With a mixture of relief, eagerness, and anxiety, I agreed immediately. That first night, we made it, if that's what it's called. I wasn't really that excited, so I wasn't able to maintain a full erection. As usual, Muriel was very warm and understanding. We wrote it off to the awkwardness of the first time. But the sexual thing never really improved. On other occasions, I felt passion in stops and starts, but I was never really able to maintain the excitement long enough. I became so unsure of myself that I had to try it with other women. There were plenty of opportunities, and happily, things went better. But I learned something: extramarital liaisons are too much of a strain on me. Although my wife didn't notice a change, I did. I have been preoccupied, ill at ease—probably feeling guilty. I've decided: no more."

*

Jane, a thirty-four-year-old former legal secretary, long believed the sex in her marriage was inadequate, but this had not distressed her until she turned thirty and began to experience an emptiness she interpreted as specifically sexual. When this happened, she felt tight, as if she would break in two; she became lethargic and began to overeat. A year later and thirty pounds heavier, Jane decided to go back to work. Her employment in a law office had a tonic effect; unlike her husband, Jack, and her stuffy neighbors, the people she met at work were talkative, intellectual, alert—her psychological equals. They stimulated her, were attentive to her, and helped assuage the disappointments in her marriage.

"It's hard to explain it exactly, but I guess what happened was that after about twelve years of marriage, I started to feel frustrated. It was like I was in heat; I started looking over every guy I met—at work especially, but even in the street. I fantasized having an affair with each of them; I imagined getting skin to skin and having him in me. Just a touch on the shoulder from a guy at work would set me off. I would get a flush that was unsettling. I don't know if what happened to me was something physical or psychological. I can empathize now with a sixteen-year-old boy who is led around by his genitals. I seemed to be single-minded.

"My husband loves me and I care for him. But making love to him, that's another issue. Something was missing you know. It was never satisfying, and although I had had sexual experience before marriage, it was not a good basis for comparison. I was so young then that I didn't really make contact with the experience. Besides, adolescent boys were so fast and self-centered that I was lucky if they would masturbate me to orgasm. In fact, things weren't so different with Jack; he'd touch me and come very quickly . . . then he'd masturbate me. But I never felt myself caring while coming. After a while, going to bed with Jack was a chore. I experienced a certain humiliation."

Surprisingly, Jane, a striking redhead with high cheekbones and smooth, pale skin, who had shed her excess weight soon after returning to work, experienced a number of rejections once she began to look for sexual partners. The men she met were her age or a little older and were not as sexually oriented as she had fantasized. Often, the men she was attracted to, particularly at work, seemed to be more interested in promoting their careers than in entering into time-consuming affairs.

One night, for instance, Jane shared a cab with Jeff, a very inventive corporate lawyer in her office. They both had been drinking heavily at an office party and he began feeling her all over; she responded immediately, but Jeff didn't pursue it. At an intimate lunch the next day, he told her he hadn't been as turned

on to a woman in years as he had been to her the previous night.
He confided that the vitality had been sapped from his own
marriage ages ago. Then, as Jane sat there astonished, he
apologized for his behavior and suggested they keep away from
each other so as not to create an uncomfortable situation at the
office. Things like this kept happening. Jane tried transferring
her sexy feelings to her husband but he wasn't very interested
either. The pattern was well formed: once a week, quickly, and
without fanfare. Out of desperation, Jane became bolder in her
approaches:

"Mostly I had to seize opportunities wherever they occurred—
in a bar, in a bus, in one of my night classes. I'd mentally size the
men up and decide which one to work on. I became an initiator.
There's nothing like it—the thrill of making a man notice me,
dropping hints, kidding. I've developed endless ways of finding
men. If a guy helps me home with packages, I always ask him up
for a drink, and one thing leads to another. I've found many men
really are on the search; my timidity was the real barrier! The
whole game of planning seductions is very exciting but I follow
two rules: I never see the same man twice and I never let my affairs keep me away from my children.

"From time to time I do wonder whether I might not be fooling around a little too much: for a while, I told myself I was trying to find a man who could make me feel like a complete
woman. I don't believe that any longer. Now that I'm into it, I
think I was looking for just what I found—the fun, excitement,
and challenge of it all, the suspense and the intrique, the hunting
around for something new. I keep occupied by having affairs.
Nothing too serious. For one thing, I'm not ready to make a
break from Jack. The funny thing is I am less demanding of him
these days and he doesn't seem to mind seeing less of me. I go off
to meet some guy or to attend my college classes and Jack just
looks up from the TV and grunts. Maybe I'm just holding on until the children are a little older. They think my husband is the
best father in the world because he is so easygoing. He lets them

get away with practically anything. I couldn't possibly disillusion them. Besides, what would a divorce solve? I'm not even sure there's a real problem."

*

The names we give the experiences just described are extramarital relations, infidelity, adultery, unfaithfulness, affairs, cheating. Women and men, men and women—the attraction between the sexes, the basic desire of the one for the other, is often not limited to the marriage partner. The human condition implies a continuous search for love and attention, sometimes diverted but sometimes rawly sought and passionately set into motion. The extramarital relationship is a tempting source of diversity and fulfillment; it is a major issue on the minds of millions of people.

Most of us take the same attitude toward extramarital sex that we take toward paying our income tax. As Morton Hunt says in his excellent book, *The Affair,* many of us cheat—some more, some less; most of us who don't would like to but are afraid; neither the actual nor the potential cheaters among us are prone to disclose the truth or defend their views except to a few confidants; and practically all of us teach our children the accepted moral code, though we neither conform to it ourselves nor expect our children to when they have grown up.

Whatever our convictions about infidelity, our fascination with it is endless, as evidenced by the popularity of the subject in movies, novels, and drama. Significantly, the adulterous activity is almost invariably portrayed as immensely enjoyable but doomed to end in tragedy. In life itself, the available facts indicate that large numbers of adulterers meet with less devastating destinies and the joys of adultery usually fall short of their literary and celluloid depictions. In any case, although we swarm to novels and movies in which adultery is a central theme, when asked about our attitude toward adultery, most of us pay lip service to the traditional code. Do we deliberately lie? Probably not; more likely we are ambivalent about it and cannot or do not know how to resolve the dilemma comfortably.

Men and Women:
Now and Then, Here and There

To be or not to be monogamous is for most married people in today's Western culture a perplexing decision, and the choice is becoming more difficult in more marriages all the time. Infidelity is on the increase. The late Dr. Alfred C. Kinsey's statistics, based largely on interviews conducted thirty years ago, revealed a remarkably high incidence. Since then, encouraged by the birth control pill and by an atmosphere of growing permissiveness concerning all sexuality, sexual roaming has increased considerably. The prevalence of the institution of marriage is matched only by the prevalence of the transgressions against it.

Through the ages, and in most cultures and societies today, there have been rules for the maintenance of the marriage system and proscriptions against breaking the rules. Yet as sociologist Gerhand Neubeck reports in his book *Extramarital Relations*, "the grass has been greener on the other side," regardless of where the turf is located—Africa, Europe, Asia, or America, in cold climates or in warm ones, among the white, black, and yellow races. There are extramarital relations in every country and on all continents. Adultery persists in the face of powerful taboos and the most stringent religious dogmas. Human desire has never been confined to the institution that narrows it, even though that institution has endured and prospered.

Despite the limitations set upon extramarital sexual relations by practically all known cultures, the definitions of the term and the means of enforcing conformity vary widely among societies. The outstanding issue in most preliterate and ancient societies was not sexual morality, even though many of us today interpret it so. Primarily adultery was considered a threat to the economic stability of a society and specifically to male property rights. Wives were property and the privileges of property owners superseded the desires of chattel. Additionally, men wanted to be sure of the genetic heritage of their heirs. The ·ancient

Hebrews, for example, were less concerned with the Seventh Commandment in a moral sense than with the necessity that a man know who his son was so he could retain economic and social power over him. Thus they severely punished adulterers, because they put a son's paternity in doubt.

Indeed, the behavior pattern designated as "marriage" would probably never have been invented if groups of men had not feared the mate-stealing of their fellow men. This concept of mate as property is readily observable among primates, the mammals most closely related to man. The males treat mates they have acquired as property to be defended against the aggressions of other males, yet both males and females have an apparent propensity to take advantage of sexual opportunities with others. With regard to men in current times, sociologist Dr. Robert N. Whitehurst's study *Extramarital Sex: Alienation or Extension of Normal Behavior* concluded it is often inevitable:

> Given certain average conditions in the married life of the males involved, it is possible to predict an adulterous outcome for a great number of males between the ages of forty and forty-five that may be created out of natural conditions arising over years of marriage. . . . Recent research shows that marriages, contrary to the togetherness notions extant in our culture, do not, through time, become characterized by increasing depth and intensiveness of marital communication. Instead, there is some evidence that time takes its toll in regard to the importance of the relationship. . . . The phenomenon of extramarital male infidelity can be conceptualized as a cultural-social problem with a high probability of involvement for many males . . . In its essence, the behavior should be quite frequently expected, and if expected and explained as a social, structural, and cultural problem, it may then be construed much more nearly as normal rather than abnormal behavior in the kind of society we now experience.

While historical, anthropological, and sociological data fail to reveal a society that has consistently suppressed and severely punished its males for extramarital relations, for females the cultural situations have been quite different. The majority of human societies that have been studied by social scientists completely prohibit and severely punish sexual relations by a married woman with anyone other than her husband. It is a rare society that freely permits women extramarital sexual relations; more usually, they are permitted under special circumstances. In an occasional society, it is the custom for a male to lend his wife to his guest. In other situations, sex is permitted, or even required, between a wife and her brother-in-law, for example, during certain religious celebrations or as part of the marriage ceremony. Yet even in these relatively rare societies with rather lenient attitudes toward female extramarital sex, such activity is tolerated only because it is not seen as a threat to the security or masculinity of husbands; after all, it is carried out under *their* rules and with *their* control.

But times have been changing, if not so much in societal restrictions, then in women's adherence to these restrictions. There has been a significant change, for example, in the incidence of extramarital sexual experience among American women: they are having sexual relationships outside their marriages by an earlier age than did women in Kinsey's time. This change has been reported in two recent reliable and large-scale studies of American sexual behavior. One study of 2,372 married women was conducted by Robert R. Bell and Dorothy-ann Peltz; the results were published in March 1974 in *Medical Aspects of Human Sexuality*. The other, a study of some 1,500 married men and women, was conducted by the Playboy Foundation and published as a book, *Sexual Behavior in the 1970's*, with a text by Morton Hunt.

In Kinsey's day, it was only by the age of forty that a little over a quarter of the women surveyed had had extramarital experience. Bell and Peltz found that such experience had been had by the same percentage of the women they surveyed by the age of thirty-five; they predicted that when all members of the group they had chosen to investigate reached forty, 40 percent of them would have had extramarital experience. The Playboy Foundation's statistics were even more startling. Their figures showed that while in Kinsey's time only 8 percent of young wives—those under age twenty-four—had reported extramarital sexual experience, by 1972, 24 percent did. Conclusion: Extramarital sex among women is rapidly approaching the male pattern.

Marriage: A Paradox

Despite the cultural restrictions against extramarital sex on the part of wives and the quasi-intolerance of the sexual affairs of husbands, the evidence is overwhelming that a great deal of adultery occurs. No marriage today is felt to be immune:

Marjorie:	You mean Al's never been off with another woman?
June:	Not as far as I know. Why should he? He seems happy.
Marjorie:	Why should he? That's a hell of a question. Why should my Martin, why should any of them?
June:	Al just doesn't seem interested in other women.
Marjorie:	How old is he?
June:	Thirty-nine.
Marjorie:	He'll be starting any day now!

Nearly everyone feels the temptation to wander sexually during married life, whether very occasionally and only in fantasy, or often and in the flesh. Longer lifespans, greater leisure, and freedom from many of the medical and economic ills that once preoccupied us have encouraged us to raise the level of our emotional aspirations. We marry early and we expect a lot more than our ancestors did from marriage—heightened sexual passion, continuous love, emotional security, stimulating companionship, thorough compatibility. Since childhood, society has impressed upon us the promise that marriage will bring total physical, emotional, and social fulfillment. For many, though, particularly those who believed the romanticized notions of what marriage would do for them, the disappointment comes quickly, passion cools, and interest wanes. The fire is banked, and as time goes by, fewer and fewer sparks are struck. The excitement of discovery, of having novel emotions and impressions, of conflict, of finding new ways of sharing, becomes more and more infrequent as mates come to know each other more fully. The marriage may become boring, stale, empty, deadly.

For some, this kind of *belle indifference* comes amazingly soon, for others it's postponed for years. Evidence indicates, however, that eventually it comes to the great majority of marriages in some degree. One major research study involving hundreds of families showed that the longer people lived together, the less satisfied with the arrangement they became. This generalization held up even for marriages that were thirty and more years old.

Monotony, the treadmill, humdrum are words that describe states of feeling from which most of us usually want to escape. This seems true whether tedium stems from eight hours on an assembly line, from eating the same food day after day, or from going through the same old motions with the same person, saying and thinking and doing similar things, endlessly. *Satiation* is the technical word for it. *Fed up* is somewhat more descriptive. This is the human condition, and it is not necessarily an indication of neuroticism or immaturity.

Even those of us whose marriages are satisfactory or genuinely happy are not protected from fantasies of infidelity. With the passage of time, this becomes increasingly true.

The face that excited, the touch that electrified, the personality that stimulated, eventually become merely comfortable, like the living-room sofa. Most of us can tolerate this for a time—we absorb ourselves in work, an avocation, our children—but as the years pass, we may experience an agonizing desperation. "Is this all there is? Am I to die without ever falling in love again?" mourns the woman, now nearing forty, whose private anguish is growing older and seeing her beauty fade. And the not so youthful, slightly paunchy man sitting next to a lovely woman on the commuter special from Connecticut can't help but wonder, "With her, could I recapture it all again?"

We all want to live the complete life: to have the security of marriage and the variety and excitement of the single life. This is difficult to do when extramarital sex is involved because the issue calls into play a fundamental human paradox: A person feels most fully alive when he can be stimulated by the challenge of the unknown and yet have the security of the known to give him the confidence he needs to try something different. The pleasure of being alive depends to a considerable degree on the ability to include both known and unknown elements in one's life, but if extramarital sex is chosen as the medium, particularly the main medium, for providing newness and excitement, the likelihood is that it will threaten the security that is a prerequisite for its appreciation.

The solutions to the marital dilemma are varied. Some people find lovers despite the risks; others experiment with group marriage; others work at finding contentment within the marriage and suppress their extramarital desires; still others don't—they divorce.

Psychologists and sociologists confronted by the marital dilemma have suggested numerous dramatic and imaginative if not always practical alternatives to traditional marriage. Robert Rimmer (author of *The Harrad Experiment* and numerous other utopian books) suggests that two couples with their children join together in a corporate marriage, pooling all their resources—sexual, emotional, and economic—in a kind of double-the-pleasure togetherness. Swedish experiments have the husbands staying home to mind the baby while the wife goes out to earn a living. Extended family networks and day-care nurseries for rearing children have been proposed; these would provide group support and companionship for children and free parents from some of the rigors of daily child care. Other advisers go further and suggest compulsory birth control and stiff prerequisites for obtaining a marriage license. Some social scientists promote open sexual agreements for all couples; others deplore this solution as neurotic and self-defeating. Even "term" contracts in marriage, lasting anywhere from five to twenty years with options for renewal, have been proposed.

Proponents of open adultery tend to be particularly dogmatic in their insistence that extramarital sex helps make marriage more permanent and enjoyable. They argue that many, if not most, divorces are caused by the desire for sexual experimentation, and that permitting sexual variety within marriage will therefore forestall or eliminate divorce. Traditionally, marriage has been defined as an arrangement that promises both permanence and exclusivity. The proponents of open sex hope to attain greater permanence than is customary these days by letting the exclusivity go.

But would sexual experimentation within marriage necessarily eliminate divorce? Martha's opening remarks to me during her first marital therapy session are pertinent here:

"We agreed to have occasional affairs provided we kept them light. My husband feels betrayed by me. His affairs had indeed been casual, but mine had become involved. He felt my love for him had become weakened or else this wouldn't have happened. It is my goal in marital therapy to get back together but he's growing very distant. He wants a divorce and, of course, I blame myself. I see that for me, affairs are dangerous because they so quickly get out of perspective."

Far from being a panacea, sexual sharing is also a threat to security because many people find it difficult or impossible to keep to the ground rules. On the other hand, some authorities, blinded to the fact that some are not only capable of functioning with extramarital allowances but seem to thrive on them, rigidly insist that this behavior is always inimical to marriage and should be fought against and squelched.

Obviously, any given solution will enhance the marital relationship of some couples and prove destructive to that of others.
The advocacy of a single specific lifestyle is useless: what may
apply to one person will not apply to another; and what is true
for one person at a particular moment in life may not be true for
that same person at a later moment. Over the centuries, we have
been offered numerous formulas by self-proclaimed saviors,
revolutionaries, prophets, behavioral scientists, and philos-
ophers, and not one of them has proved ideal for all. Ideal
solutions exist only in an ideal world; in the real world, the best
we can do is seek options that fit our individual natures and do
not violate our cherished values. In this society, and with our
emotional equipment, group marriage or open sexual sharing
produces jealousy and conflict for most of us. Though these solutions work for some people, they hardly help the majority who
live in a conventional marriage contend with the tensions and
anxieties of adultery.

Strains of Straying

The German philosopher, Schopenauer, told the story of two
porcupines huddled together on a cold winter's night. The
temperature dropped; the animals moved closer together. But
then there was a problem: each kept getting "stuck" by the
other's quills. Finally, with much shifting and shuffling in changing positions, they managed to work out an equilibrium whereby
each got maximum warmth with a minimum of painful pricking
from the other. Many husbands and wives have something in
common with the huddling porcupines. They want to achieve
and maintain a kind of equilibrium; warmth and closeness, but
without the sometimes agonizing "pricking" that comes from
continuous interaction with another human being.

Adultery as a means to "smooth the rub" is a high-risk undertaking, particularly for a person who is fairly happy in general

and relatively satisfied with his marriage. Probably only a small percentage of men and women in our society have fully freed themselves of deep-seated anxieties and guilts about extramarital sex relations, and still fewer have mates who are similarly free. If the unfaithful partner is free of anxiety and guilt, he or she is still concerned about being dishonest with a mate who would disapprove if the truth were known. And even where reciprocal knowledge and approval exist, frequent or extended extramarital sexual activities can produce negative effects on marital and personal happiness by draining time, energy, money, affection, and other resources from the marriage.

Some men and women enter into an affair confident that there is very little chance of being found out. Yet feelings about the outside relationship cannot help but affect behavior within the marriage. The signals may be ever so slight and subtle—an inability to concentrate, a fleeting and mysterious smile as thoughts of the lover flit through the mind, periods of inattentiveness to the spouse followed by unusually fierce demonstrations of affection—but the perceptive partner will notice these new behaviors and in time begin to wonder. As one woman expressed it:

"He just started acting . . . differently. Nothing I could really put my finger on, but it bothered me and then suddenly the thought jumped into my mind, 'He's having an affair!' When I asked him about it, he told me the truth and my whole life came crashing down around me. I thought we had so much going for us and then I came to this hideous realization that the person I thought I was married to wasn't the person I was really married to at all."

Immediate feelings of pain and anger usually result in the stipulation that the straying mate either end the outside involvement or leave; occasionally, a husband or wife will attempt to adjust to the partner's affair. "She's a good wife and mother, all in all," one man told me. "And maybe I haven't the right to insist she stop seeing the guy she is sleeping with, since it doesn't seem to affect *our* relationship all that much." But in a later conversation with this same man, he confessed to me that, "It just can't work. I go to the office every day and I sit there wondering whether she's with him. I imagine them in bed together. It's torture."

Nor do the problems end here. Suppose this man's wife had not been discovered but found herself sexually charged by the affair. What does she do with her drive? How does she cope with the powerful feelings that dominate her but cannot be shared with her husband? If she tries to share them, how can she help comparing one man to another—and if her husband is found wanting, what does she do with her feelings? Bury them and bury too her newly-kindled sexual responsiveness? Or, respecting her natural right to those feelings, does she embark on a succession of affairs? Or does she divorce her husband?

Probably what underlies the most severe anxieties concerning our mate's extramarital sex is a fear that we are losing control: control of our spouse, control of the relationship, control of the future, control of ourselves. This fear of loss of control rooted in insecurity is quite common today. As we lose control of other sectors of our lives (or discover we never really had control), we wish all the more to be secure in our intimate relationships and our family life. If things are unstable elsewhere—at work, in our country generally—the stability of the home becomes all the more important.

This fear of the loss of our partner's emotional bond, of the love, affection, and support he or she provides, can be terrifying. It is to insure ourselves against these anxieties that we consent to ethical proscriptions of extramarital sex. When we suspect our mates of transgressing this agreement, we become anxious and defensive. We assume that if we lose our mate, it will be to someone else; consequently, we begin to view others with suspicion. Such behavior makes us less attractive, it promotes aloofness and tension in our marital partner, and, as in a self-fulfilling prophecy, we become more suspicious and our basic fear of loss deepens.

An example may illustrate the problem more clearly. In

marriage therapy, one frequently sees both spouses engaging in behavior they consider the most appropriate reaction to some wrong the other is doing. For instance, a wife may have the impression that her husband is not open enough for her to know where she stands with him, what is going on in his head, what he is doing when he is away from home, and so on. Quite naturally, she will therefore attempt to make herself more secure by asking him questions, watching his behavior, and checking on him in a variety of other ways. He is likely to consider her behavior intrusive and react by withholding from her information that in and by itself would be quite harmless and irrelevant—"just to teach her that I am not a child in need of checking." Rather than making her back down, her husband's reaction increases her insecurity and provides further fuel for her worries and her distrust: "If he does not even talk to me about these little things, he *must* be hiding something." The less information he gives her, the more persistently will she seek it, and the more she seeks it, the less he will give her. It is not long before the drama evolves to a point that Dr. Paul Watzlawick and his associates describe in their book, *Change*, as reminiscent of two sailors hanging out of either side of a sailboat in order to steady it: the more the one leans overboard, the more the other has to hang out to compensate for the instability created by the other's attempts at stabilizing the boat, while the boat itself would be quite steady if not for the insecurities of its passengers. It is predictable that unless something changes in this situation, the occupants of the (marriage) boat will be under constant unnecessary strain, or worse yet, finish up in the water.

There is very little doubt that extramarital sexual relations—particularly if frequent—complicate a marital relationship. Does this mean that the adulterers are then immoral, bad, or evil? Clearly not. For the evidence from in-depth studies such as that conducted by Morton Hunt mentioned earlier shows that although in many circumstances an extramarital affair severely damages the marriage and family, in other circumstances it is of no consequence; and in still other circumstances it may awaken an individual to his emotional needs and capabilities or cause the end of a fraudulent, unsatisfactory marriage and allow both partners to pursue healthier options.

Those who choose to remain faithful are confronted with drawbacks as well as rewards. Some, even though unsatisfactorily married, forgo both infidelity and divorce because of severe self-doubt, or for religious, social, or ethical reasons. Their penalty is frustration and unhappiness. Yet there are rewards: their choice leaves them secure and easy in conscience. In other words, they are unhappy but comfortable.

Others, though suffering equally from unmet desires and dissatisfactions, sublimate these desires, redirecting them into compulsive work, homemaking, or similar activities. They do not dare to explore and therefore will never be disrupted but excited by the discovery of an unsuspected sexual-emotional facet to their personalities. But this choice, also has its reward; a productive output that is more socially and personally acceptable than illicit sex and love.

Some people work hard at their marriage and are fortunate enough to achieve a happy, satisfying union. They have few unmet needs and remain faithful with little effort. Even the desire for "something new" is relatively weak and passes or is directed back toward their mates without great difficulty.

On the other side, a large and growing number of people decide to take the chance and defy the monogamous code. They too share a mixed bag of advantages and disadvantages. For them, the extramarital experience may have many different kinds of impact and effect, ranging from disastrous to beneficial.

I believe, along with Morton Hunt and others, that each extramarital act ought not be prejudged as morally evil or morally good but rather considered for its effects on a continuum from destructive to useful. That is, each individual should weigh his or her decision to have an affair or not according to the motivating circumstance, the kind of extramarital relationship engaged in, and the effects on all concerned. It is the responsibility of each of us to take into account our own needs, those of our mate and children, and the probable effects of our acts on all connected with us. The choice is not up to society, it is our own.

Accepting responsibility for this choice is like traveling in a strange country without a guide to point out what we should see, or even more worrisome, without a road map to tell us how to get there. Becoming one's own ultimate judge is no easy task, but the alternatives—conforming to arbitrary social rules or submitting to frustration and conflict—are much more disheartening.

The purpose of this book is to help with the journey. It is intended for those people touched or troubled by, or just plain curious about, extramarital sexual behavior. The intention is to assist the reader to make a considered decision regarding extramarital behavior and to provide a resource in those instances where the choice that has been made is not working well.

Types of Affairs

Light 'n' Heavy

"When I travel or go to an out-of-town business meeting, it is my custom to seek out a woman to share my bed. It's novel, it's exciting. An hour, a day, or a week later, I say good-bye and return to my family. Sometimes I think of a lover for a week or two after the encounter. We may even work it out to meet again from time to time. But although I am flirtatious, playful, and I come on pretty aggressively, I think it is also apparent that I am distant. I never let myself fall in love with any of the women nor do I think any of them have ever really fallen for me. This is deliberate. Aside from the fact that my primary commitment is to my wife, I am very busy. I couldn't handle any more than an occasional fling. There are even times when I'm away from home and too busy to fit it in. Of course, if I could have a woman delivered to my room, I wouldn't turn it down. But to go searching and go through the wining and dining thing—sometimes I just can't be bothered. With me, the issue is unencumbered sex, rubbing up against new flesh. If it gets burdensome, forget it. I have enough of that already."

*

"Sex to me isn't just a roll in the hay. It's very important. When I first met Barry seven years ago and he came on to me with his sexual liberation line and 'let's get it together' and all that, I quickly straightened him out. He felt rejected and pretty insulted. My reaction was he got what his hand called for! Over the next year or so we continued to run into each other with our respective spouses at social gatherings. Then my husband suggested we invite Barry and his wife to dinner. I went along with this and we began to see more of them. I had this vague feeling of discomfort back then when this was occurring. What happened to me was that I was falling for this guy. Knowing me, this spelled trouble because when I fall, I really plunge. And that's what has happened. Barry and I have been linked romantically for five years now. I see him on the average of three or four times a week. We still get together socially with our mates, although not as often as several years ago. Neither Barry nor I encourage it. It's not a comfortable scene. Even after all these years and tons of rationalizations, being in that situation still feels fraudulent. My hope is that one day we will each untie our present marital knots and live together openly as husband and wife."

*

It is apparent from these two descriptions that to speak as though extramarital relationships were all alike is a simplification. Marital infidelity ranges from the occasional one-night stand to the once-in-a-lifetime *grand amour*. The types of affairs men and women choose vary in their implications and consequences both for the person and the marriage. Indeed, for an activity admitting of such diversity it would be possible to draw up a systematic matrix including many combinations of duration, seriousness, and intensity, and discuss each category separately. Although this would be a thorough approach, it would be unnecessarily complicated, for stripped to their basics, types of affairs come down to this: those of relatively low emotional involve-ment and those of higher emotional involvement. These are the two broad categories discussed in this chapter.

Never Become Serious

Generally, in low-involvement affairs, meetings are sporadic, or if frequent, scarcely add to or deepen the relationship.

Of least significance here is the kind of relationship that takes the form of coquetry. This includes the normal flirting and minor conquests that are part of every social gathering. Conceivably more serious in its implications for the marriage is the one-night stand—sex as play, a sometime thing that usually leaves little residue except guilt. More regular meetings may take the form the French label *la matinée*. This is a playful relationship between working men and women who use the lunch hour or after work "relaxation period" for their rendezvous. The basic rule for such a relationship is "Never become serious." The hazards are being found out and that one partner might fall in love and thus become serious.

Casual sexual experiences may occur in marriages described as good as well as in those termed bad or difficult. The in-dividuals may be liberal or conservative, straitlaced or perennial "chaser" types, rich or poor. Although sometimes the product of a meticulous plan, these affairs are often spontaneous pairings of the moment. They may be highly pleasurable or the reality may fall far short of fantasy. As the adulterous heroine of Erica Jong's *Fear of Flying* asks in a moment of satiric bitterness, "Why is it all so complicated? Why do you have to risk your whole life for one measly zipless fuck?" All sorts of things can go wrong: the pair-ing may be poor (a partner may prove inconsiderate or inade-quate); illicit sex, counter to our society's mythology, may be discovered to be an inhibition rather than an aphrodisiac; guilt and anxiety may enter the drama; the motel, apartment, or whatever may turn out to be seedy, unsuitable, distasteful, etc. In general, though, even when a brief extramarital encounter has not been altogether pleasurable, many people feel pleased with themselves for having had the experience.

Randolph, a forty-seven-year-old psychologist, looks placid, content, and uncomplicated. His features are sharp and clean. His hair is graying, giving him a distinctive appearance, and he dresses well but conservatively. His tastes and many of his convictions stem from a conservative base. Over the past several years his conservatism has been slowly dissolving. In fact, he is rather proud of his departures from orthodoxy. Raised in a comfortable Irish Catholic suburb on Long Island, he became an agnostic during his college days. This was perhaps his most difficult and profound life change because religion had played a major role in his childhood. Forsaking beliefs that to some extent had guided his life called for a dramatic psychic reorganization. Characteristically, Randolph had worked at restructuring his "life rules" in a cautious, deliberate manner. It was many years before he felt as comfortable with himself as he did when his religious beliefs were strong.

Randolph attended Harvard for eight consecutive years until attaining his doctorate in experimental psychology. He was more thing-oriented in those days—designing elaborate apparatuses and complex animal experiments was his forte. He rejected working with people—psychotherapy—because psychotherapists were "soft-headed" scientists who dealt with intangibles. This, too, changed over the years as Randolph took further training, and he eventually became a clinical psychologist. It was during his last year at Harvard that Randolph met his wife Jean, then an editor of a popular weekly magazine in the Boston area. Her attraction for Randolph was immediate. After two years of dating regularly, they married. Soon after they were married, Randolph was drafted and shipped overseas. Though he was away from her for months at a time, he never went prowling in search of another woman; in fact, he even had a difficult time envisioning the unfaithful act. In the early years of his marriage, if confronted at a party by a tempting body, he refused to let go and speculate on what it would be like to test that unknown flesh. But after several years of marriage, when Jean took their daughter Jennifer for a six-week summer visit to her folks in Austria, desire tormented him in the night and he consciously decided on an affair.

"When I decided to try finding someone I went out to bars where there was a friendly atmosphere and I'd meet all sorts of women. I was getting a lot of attention and I loved it. I was shy and inhibited in my teens and throughout most of my life. Until I met Jean at Harvard and fell in love with her, I had had no real romance. Now I was going out and I was really excited—and scared, very scared. One Sunday night I met a waitress who was very pretty, very warm, and very sexy. She must have been forty-five but she looked much younger. She was married but separated for the past five months. She was also horny as hell but I didn't know that at first. She was a real lady— pleasant and proper. She seemed to enjoy my company without having anything else in mind. Overcoming my reserve, I asked her to dinner. She accepted. It was nice but I couldn't make my move—I asked her out again for the next night, and this time, although I wasn't sure what she had in mind for later, I knew what I had in mind. After dinner we went to my place and in a short time we were in a passionate position on the couch and decided to move into the bedroom. Once we undressed, things didn't go too well. I was so uptight I couldn't maintain my erection. Damn it, it was just as I've told my patients—'The harder you try the softer it gets.'

"The irony of it all! All I could think of was, 'Doctor, heal thyself' but it wasn't easy. I know it must have been terrifically frustrating for her also, but she was understanding. Maybe she was used to it—who knows? In any case, I wasn't about to get into any long conversations about it. She wanted to stay over-night but, partially out of awkwardness and embarrassment about striking out sexually, I insisted on taking her home.

"The next day she called me and suggested we spend the eve-ning together. When she said that, I got a sudden pang of anxiety but I decided to go ahead with it and arranged to see her. This time we got it on sexually. After meeting a few more times, though, another problem developed: I found it almost impossible to talk to her. Carrying on an extended conversation was actually painful. My interests were over her head, while hers were boring to me. Plus, and probably more important, I didn't want to put the effort into a heavy conversation. So, since we couldn't stay in bed all the time, we began to feel ill at ease with each other. After a couple of weeks of having seen each other for a total of six or seven evenings, our 'relationship' was over. It died a natural death. I think both of us knew from the start that this was a passing thing. There was never any talk of 'What do I mean to you?' or 'What are we going to do about all this?' or any of that commitment jazz. There was no entanglement. For me, that was fine. It was mostly the physical part that mattered to me. The interplay of personalities would have been nice had she been more compatible, but truthfully, it's just as well. The last thing I'd want is a real involvement. But I learned something: without some sort of involvement, the effort may not be worth it. It's a paradox; I don't need, nor do I really think it's wise, to get involved, yet a relationship based on nothing but sex is too limited. Granted, this time it was pretty good but that's because it was such a novel experience. Looking to the future, I really don't see myself doing this sort of thing.

"There's one wild aspect to this experience that really unnerved me. I wrote Jean a couple of notes during the time of my brief affair. One night she called and just as the conversation was ending, she said, 'Oh, by the way, dear, your Freudian slip is showing.' She refused to explain that. She just giggled. When she returned home in August I questioned her about that odd remark and she showed me the note I had written to her. The last line read, 'Wish you were her.' I was almost floored! After a forced laugh, I changed the subject. There was no way I was going to touch that!"

The lack of emotional involvement in Randolph's affair is not atypical. Occasional affairs such as these are probably the most common. When half the husbands and a quarter of the wives in the Kinsey studies acknowledged that they had had at least one overt extramarital affair, most of them were referring to the shorter, lighter affair. In many instances, one or both lovers take deliberate steps to keep the affair limited. The strategies vary and include dating several people simultaneously so as not to lean on one too heavily; breaking off as soon as feelings get out of hand; setting limiting ground rules; deliberately alienating a lover who is pushing unwanted intimacy; and cutting down on meetings when emotional vulnerability becomes an issue. Of course, the away-from-home affair has many of these safeguards built in and is a favorite with those seeking low involvement. The primary purpose of these strategies is to keep one's real life private; by not disclosing themselves, the lovers seek to avoid intimacy and vulnerability.

Sometimes, though, people who avoid emotional intimacy in casual affairs are manifesting a more general style of relating. These people are usually uninvolved in their marriages also. Again, the strategies vary. Men commonly escape not only in affairs but in work and sports; women, in addition to pursuing affairs, may take shelter in household responsibilities, work, hobbies, and similar activities. Frequently, the occasional affair is a kind of palliative for an aching marriage; it eases the pain without curing anything. That is just what some people want. They may lack the emotional apparatus for an intimate marriage relationship. They remain married mainly for security and companionship, or because marriage offers an established social role, a home base, children, and the rewards of being part of a family. When a marriage such as this breaks up, it is usually not because the occasional affairs stunted marital intimacy—that was lacking all along—but because one mate wanted the intimacy and warmth the other would not permit. If both partners do not miss or need high involvement, the pattern of casual affairs may go on for many years without disrupting the marriage.

If a casual affair is not likely to have much effect on an uninvolved marriage, what does it do to an intimate marriage? This is very difficult to determine because the effects are varied and complex. For one thing, a loving, satisfying, and close marriage relationship, although it does not preclude extramarital sexual involvement, decreases its likelihood. One plausible generalization, though, is that an outside involvement will cause much greater strain in an intimate marriage than in a low-involvement marriage.

Diane, a heavy blond woman who is visibly graying, appears to be in her early forties. She has been married eighteen years and describes here a period of her life when she had two casual affairs.

"Although these sexual experiences were meaningful to me, they were far from dramatic. I did not experience a grand awakening and I wasn't particularly enamored of my sexual partners. Yet I was excited and there was a change in me that I thought I was concealing successfully. I wasn't. One Sunday morning my husband turned to me in bed and said, 'I know people change as they grow, but when you live with a woman for such a long time, you get to know her very well; you relate to me in a certain way. In the past few months, a change has come over you. I don't know what to make of it. I don't know what's wrong, but you don't seem to be with me in the same way. Did I do something to provoke this?' "

This kind of repercussion does not always occur in an intimate marriage. Some affairs may go undiscovered and even add to the individual and to the marriage. Nonetheless, the adulterous party takes a greater risk in an involved marriage. If the outside intimacy is sensitive as well as sexual, there will probably be subtle changes in personality and these are more likely to be detected in an intimate marriage. Typically, at this juncture the adulterous mate will begin to lie: "Oh, it's my business troubles," or "I'm just edgy, I need a rest." If his mate does not buy these ambiguous answers, and suspicion continues to be aroused, the marriage will probably deteriorate.

The *Grand Amour*

In my experience the majority of men and women who believed their affairs were of minor consequence to their marriages described these affairs as shallow and short-lived, or enduring but emotionally limited. Moreover, most of these people seemed to have marriages that were also emotionally limited. Responses were less positive and more flavored with conflict when the marriage was characterized by high involvement. When the affair was described as highly involved—that is, the lovers were sexually, emotionally, and intellectually attuned—their reflections on the experience were usually emotionally charged and filled with conflict.

Celia, a lively, attractive nurse with a slim but voluptuous figure, has been married to Joseph for twelve years. They have two children aged nine and four. Joseph is a successful, soft-spoken attorney who, in contrast to Celia's rather brash, agitated manner, gives the impression of sincerity and of being a take-life-as-it-comes sort of guy. Celia agrees with this description and adds:

"Joseph is solid and stable but he lacks something important. There is a certain excitement missing. He is predictable, practical, and proper. That's Joseph. There is no mystery; that certain impishness, growth potential, adventurousness is lacking. It's hard to pin down, but whatever it is, Justin has it. He's complex; you're never sure what he's going to do next. There's intensity and mystery. His eyes look out, but they also look in."

Celia met Justin three years ago in a therapy group just after she had her youngest child. Their mutual love did not come suddenly and irresistibly; it grew slowly as each of them became aware of the attraction and voluntarily continued an association bound to evolve into an affair.

After eighteen months, Celia's love for Justin was all-encompassing, a synthesis of romantic passion and motherly tenderness. This was a love that grew not by absence and imagination but by nearness, merging, and sharing of experiences. At first, both Justin and Celia tried to suppress the enormity of their attraction for each other by reassuring themselves that what they felt was physical desire or mere infatuation. This didn't hold up. The evidence of their feelings and actions was too strong for them to continue seeing their affair as merely a type of friendship supplemental to their marriages, but to admit that this was a potentially exclusive relationship would be acknowledging that their marriages were indeed endangered. There would be heightened disruption and instability in their lives until the conflict between the affair and marriage was resolved. Unlike the casual affair, which may coexist with the marriage, the high-involvement affair competes with it directly. Celia continues:

"Justin and I phoned each other constantly. We saw each other three or four times a week. We were always on each other's minds. I became like an army commander, always prepared for every contingency. I knew exactly which restaurants to avoid because they were too big, noisy, and popular, and which to avoid because they were too small, quiet, and compromising. I became an expert on where to get my hair cut, washed, and set in record time and where to buy children's clothes without spending hours rummaging through stacks of mis-sized items. I had friends who could cover for me on days the housekeeper was sick; friends to help account for the sudden presence in my drawer of an expensive gift from Justin ('Let's say *you* gave me this brooch. No, not gave. Why would you have given it to me? There isn't any special occasion. Let's say you know someone who is in the wholesale jewelry business and you got it for me at a third of its real price.'); friends who would tell me about movies they had seen down to the minutest details so that my reports to Joseph would be beyond question.

"Everyone in our circle—except, of course, Joseph—knew about Justin. No one approved, but no one would ever say a word to Joseph. They too knew him as a nice fellow, a sincere guy. None of them wanted to hurt him; to be the bearer of cruel tidings. Besides, people rationalized that things would be okay and that our marriage would survive. Justin and I weren't that optimistic. We realized that our marriages might be wrecked in the process. I suppose we both had our private thoughts about that—the guilt of breaking up a family; sizing up the emotional and security factors involved; considering money matters. I live comfortably, and realistically I know I wouldn't be happy to skimp and watch myself. We were, at base, scared. These thoughts were always present for me and for Justin also, although frequently they deferred to the passion of the moment.

"I recall an incident that occurred about a year ago. Justin and I managed to get away for a week in Puerto Rico. It was marvelous. Knowing that Justin had this thing about using every minute efficiently, I didn't interfere with his elaborate and detailed planning and went along with him on all the activities he chose. One day was a disaster, though. I wanted to go on a tour with him and he had other plans for us; I insisted, and he became more and more upset. He literally ended up in bed under the covers. When we talked it over later, he said that what bothered him so much was that he took our conflict as an indication that we could never live together harmoniously. He was so shaken by that projection that he felt ill. This is what I mean by a fear that loomed in the back of our minds—'will it work; will it last; am I risking my marriage only to lose everything?' That sort of thing.

"Just as our affair was disruptive, it was also constructive and rewarding. Justin and I would make love and then lie side by side and talk for two or three hours and then make love again. We discussed the books we were reading, movies we had seen, the shape the country was in, my hopes and work aspirations, his work. We talked about our childhoods, our parents, our friends, our children. Each of us came to know almost everything the other was thinking and doing every day. We were childlike and we were serious, silly and intense—we were everything. When we were together the world stood still. Time stopped. It escalated and escalated until it was so emotionally intense, intellectually stimulating, and sexually arousing that it became the best thing each of us had ever known."

The conventional notion of highly emotional affairs is that such relationships follow a cycle: intense infatuation with a new person, a relatively quick decline in passion, disillusionment, dissolution, infatuation with a new partner, and a repetition of the cycle. Certainly plenty of affairs fit this model, particularly since enormous emotional resources are required to lead two lives. As one woman, involved in a close relationship of two years, put it:

"I broke it off with Roger because I had built up a lot of resentment toward him over the two years. Conducting the affair had been more taxing for me than for him. I have children, lots of home responsibilities. He was on a much looser schedule. He was filling up free time with me, whereas I was sandwiching him into a very crowded life. It was restrictive. I never wanted to go on vacations, because I was afraid to be out of contact with Roger. I was always slipping away to make long-distance phone calls. My life was filled with subterfuge and it was no longer any fun. I couldn't relax; I couldn't get any rest. I had to make a choice, and since Roger would not make a firm commitment ('I don't think I could adjust to your children; let's just try weekends at first'), I chose my marriage."

This brings up another point. One reason high-involvement affairs are not that common is more practical than psychological: it is simply too difficult for most married people to steal away for more than a few hours a week. So although there may be a large number of people who dream of a *grand amour*, they simply cannot find the time to realize one.

But this is not the whole story. In some prolonged, involved relationships, the cycle of infatuation, heightened emotion, decline, and dissolution is no more present than it is in a good number of marriages. These relationships, like marriage, sometimes move from vitality and a strong erotic attachment to a more matter-of-fact comfortable kind of interaction. That is, they move to a level of involvement that is manageable. Surprisingly enough, some of these relationships settle into the kind of apathy that makes one wonder why they go on since there are no institutional obligations involved. But perhaps for some people sentiment and a quiescent kind of attachment are stronger than external social sanctions. Moreover, it is precisely because of their lowered intensity that these affairs can be carried on for a long time (sometimes as long as the marriage itself) without becoming threatening to the marriage. Sometimes they are a primary factor in keeping a borderline marriage intact.

In one form of arrangement of this sort, the man is married, financially secure, and has no desire to see the affair evolve into a marriage since his marriage is quite tolerable and would be expensive to terminate. The woman is usually younger, either single or divorced, and desirous of a marriage commitment. The stability and endurance of the relationship is contingent on the woman's acceptance of the current limits of the involvement while maintaining her fantasy of marriage in the future. "When my last child goes off to college" and "As soon as my wife becomes more independent" are the kinds of statements she hangs on to keep her hopes alive.

Although there are a few exceptions, an affair of deep *mutual* involvement that continues over a number of years takes a mighty toll on both the lovers and the mate, or mates if both are married. Again, the level of marital involvement is an important consideration. Other factors (such as personal maturity) being equal, generally the closer the marital relationship, the greater the strain of the extraneous involvement. The adulterer's continual absences, excuses, lack of interest, and diminished sexual appetite will be sorely resented.

As an example of the direction this tension may take, consider the period when the unfaithful spouse attempts, whether out of guilt or compassion, to repair and revitalize the marriage. This saving effort may include attempts at talking things out—not the affair, but the voids in the relationship, the differences between the partners. He or she may suggest a long vacation together, "just the two of us, without the children." The affair-involved spouse may make overt or covert resolutions to be more loving, more tolerant, more giving. Usually these maneuvers don't work. Either the faithful spouse's suspicion, mistrust, and resentment are too intense to be dismissed by promises, or the unfaithful spouse is still committed to the affair and is making a transparently feeble effort at reconciliation. In other instances, the adulterous mate is involved in self-deception. His efforts to talk things out and rekindle the marital relationship are a mask for the opportunity to criticize and emphasize shortcomings in his mate as justification for his divided loyalties.

As the marital clashes increase in intensity, becoming more venomous and destructive, they affect the adulterous lovers. Rather than drawing closer, they find themselves at each other's throats. Celia's experience is common:

"When Justin and I were feeling pressured or a conflict was raging at home, a great deal of tension and animosity developed between us. As the clashes increased in intensity and frequency at home, rather than consoling each other, we frequently made things worse. Our efforts to recapture earlier satisfaction paid off mostly when tensions at home were in remission."

Endings

Celia and Justin had, at best, moderately close marriages; although they had several mutual interests and found their mates' company pleasant, if not stimulating, their marriages were not intimate. In contrast, their relationship with each other was extremely intimate. Unlike casual affairs, which may waste away and die quietly, affairs as intense as theirs die hard.

In the uninvolved casual affair, there is very little reward other than sexual pleasure. As alluring as this is, it is usually not enough to sustain a relationship. When the novelty wears off and the conquest is assured, interest begins to wane. Because of the lack of emotional involvement, parting is usually painless and without significant consequence to the marriage. Even when the meaning of the sexual act itself is highly significant to the individual, the breakup of a casual extramarital relationship is not usually disruptive to the marriage.

Through a casual sexual encounter an individual may become awakened to aspects of himself or herself or to aspects of the marital relationship that never surfaced before. For example, one woman found, after a brief sexual encounter, that she was more sexual and more orgastic than she had ever dreamed possible. A man discovered that sexual acts his wife found distasteful and perverted were merely idiosyncratic. His extramarital sexual activity was an important experiential confirmation that his desires were not odd or "sick," as his wife had termed them. He felt better about himself and his sexuality as a result. Another person concluded after several affairs that her mate was the best all-around partner she could ever hope for. In these instances, if there is an effect on the marriage, it is not so much the extramarital *relationship* as the extramarital *experience* that serves as the disruptive or enhancing force. When this is the case, breaking up the extraneous relationship is not usually a critical incident because it was the experience rather than the person that was significant.

If breaking up is relatively painless in the casual encounter, the opposite is true in the *grand amour* where the person, rather than being incidental, is everything. Caught in a conflict between desire and obligation, between fulfillment and guilt, the adulterous mate suffers enormously and frequently manifests physical symptoms of his inner struggle. Torn between lover and mate, some individuals cannot sleep or sleep fitfully; others cannot eat or eat constantly; some take to excess drinking or to tranquilizers; many become plagued by gastrointestinal and/or other psychosomatic disorders. Work suffers, household chores pile up, the children are ignored. Frequently depression ensues. All of these symptoms deteriorate both the marriage and the affair. In such situations, it is imperative to make a decision, and paradoxically, impossible to do so.

The experience was described by one man as sitting on a picket fence, feeling the painful inner probe, but not daring to move. This man became withdrawn and preoccupied. His bills went unpaid, he began to snipe at old friends, he considered leaving a well-paying position and moving. He wanted to start over; he wanted to kill himself; he didn't know what he wanted; he sought escape. He did not want to choose between his lover and his wife, yet he knew it was necessary for him to make a decision and act on it.

In an emotion-filled conversation, Justin described his parting with Celia and its consequences for his marriage:

"I knew a choice had to be made. My marriage couldn't stand the conflict. Probably the most difficult aspect of this whole period was the necessity for concealing my pain. I was feeling so awful but I had to keep a lid on it because there was no way to account for these feelings to my family. I thought I would explode! While the decision to give up on my relationship with Celia in favor of my marriage relieved some of this agony, the loss and sorrow lasted for some time. There was also anger. Even though my wife's complaints and dissatisfactions about my being away from home so much and being preoccupied were very legitimate, I found myself blaming her for my dilemma. I realize that's crazy. She's a pretty decent person and she had a right to be dissatisfied. Things had been lousy between us during the affair. After my breakup with Celia, the problem was that I found myself acting in a way that would eventually destroy what was left of my marital relationship. That scared me; I would lose everything. But I went on, almost as if I didn't care. Between bouts of nastiness there were times when I would buy flowers and go through all sorts of romantic rituals. Then back to nastiness. This went on for about eight months before I settled down. If my wife wasn't such an exceptionally tolerant, easy-going person, there's no way our relationship would have lasted."

Of course, the conflict that an enduring high-involvement affair creates can go in another direction. It may lead to the dissolution of the marriage. Laura Greenstaff describes her experience:

"I was pretty unhappy in my first marriage. It was more a business arrangement than a relationship. We were so busy with our separate interests and responsibilities that we hardly noticed each other. There were no real fights or even strong disagreements. On the contrary, there was a lack of any strong feelings. It's not that I expected heart palpitations every time I was in my husband's presence. I'm not that much of a romantic! But there was nothing. It was a very passive relationship, almost completely lacking in passion.

"My relationship with Harold, a business acquaintance of my husband, developed over a period of five years. As the years passed, it became more and more satisfying; more and more, my emotions became invested in Harold. We fussed over each other, there was a marvelous physical relationship, and, most important of all, we had emotional compatibility. It was beautiful. I don't regard it as dirty. Actually, when it seemed that Harold and I were seriously involved and meant to continue our involvement, I left my husband. I have no real regrets about my decision but I do feel very sorry and guilty for breaking up our home and inflicting pain on my family."

Old Love or New?

What accounts for the decision to stay with the marriage or to forsake it in favor of a new love? This is the type of question that cannot be answered fully. Even those doing the choosing are not able to unravel all the variables. For those who choose to stay with their mate, it may be a matter of security—financial and emotional. Guilt, obligation, loyalty, and duty to one's children or one's religion are also common factors. At a basic level, it may be that the marriage, although not fully satisfying, is not devoid of satisfaction. For even an incomplete and flawed marriage may after the close scrutiny that conflict demands, become more practical and less romantic. This was the case with Justin. He recoginized that although Celia is a more exciting woman than his wife, their relationship would prove unworkable in the long run; along with her vibrancy, Celia possessed a volatility and self-centeredness that would make a harmonious living arrangement very hard work—too hard for Justin's taste.

When the marriage is ended in favor of the affair, it is most likely because it was seriously deteriorating anyway and the lover promised, in addition to sexual satisfaction, emotional nourishment. Frequently the affair-involved individual is strongly monogamous and became involved with a lover because of long-standing deprivation in the marriage. When love blossoms, the marriage rapidly becomes intolerable and the individual, in dissolving the marriage, is acting to restore his integrity as much as choosing greater satisfaction.

Implications

There you have it—affairs, like marriages, range from low to high involvement and, similarly, from neutral to grave in consequences. What kind of generalizations can we make from all of this?

In summary: if an individual is strongly monogamous, he or she is not likely to have an affair except out of sheer desperation. If this occurs, there is a high probability that the marriage will be ended. This likelihood increases if the lover is suitable and available. In contrast, if an individual is not particularly restrained by the monogamous code, he or she will probably have more casual affairs.

If the marriage is not a close one, these affairs may be unnoticed and without consequence. They may even have the positive consequence of keeping a marriage that is satisfactory in most respects alive and intact. If the marriage is a close one, a strain is likely to develop even if the affairs are casual—how great a strain depends on the personality of the faithful mate and how much time the extraneous involvements take from the marriage.

Of course, even if the affair is casual and the lover is not valued, the experience itself may have a personal impact with consequences for the marriage. These consequences are very complex and range from destructive to enhancing. The *grand amour*, the deep involvement, the all-encompassing affair, is a paradox: a once-in-a-lifetime experience, it is also agonizing and the riskiest of all. In the close, involved marriage, it is nearly always a disaster. In marriages that are not close, it is likely to be a continuing source of conflict, if not the beginning of the end.

Lust and Beyond
Motivations for Extramarital Affairs

Self-Deception or Self-Conception?

Why do people seek extramarital sexual experiences? Love, of course, is the most popularized reason. On screen and in novels it is portrayed as taking us unaware, capturing us, and causing us, as if shot by Cupid's arrow, to fall helplessly into another's arms. In real life, though, researchers and investigative interviewers find love a rather uncommon cause of infidelity.

What, then, does account for the proliferation of extramarital sex? There is, of course, no single or simple answer; each extramarital affair is the result of a complex interplay of forces. Members of the psychological professions are divided as to whether neurotic personality characteristics or normal and even healthy traits are primarily responsible for adulterous behavior. Some psychologists and psychiatrists who take the former position believe that people are adulterous because they were conditioned by childhood experiences to be unable to form deep commitments, or because they are so immature that they can acknowledge no limit to their needs or can acquire no realistic perspective on what to expect from marriage.

Curiously enough, Freudian-oriented professionals, those supposedly responsible for unleashing the permissive sexual outlook, generally regard practically all extramarital activity as symptomatic of pathological personality traits such as psychosexual immaturity, narcissism, character disorder, and Oedipal conflict. The evidence they present for their view comes from clinical practice with impotent men seeking potency; nonassertive, browbeaten mates who feel like worthy people only outside their marriages; couples embroiled in long-standing hostility who use cheating as a weapon; men and women who do not feel worthy of respect unless they are continually "proving" they are by new sex-love conquests; and pathologically insecure, jealous husbands and wives who drive their mates into another's arms by their constant badgering.

Of course, as has been frequently pointed out about Freud's and other psychoanalysts' conclusions about human behavior, it is not entirely legitimate for a therapist to investigate the lives of individuals who seek help for a particular disturbance and then make sweeping generalizations about the motives of all people. Yet, it is indisputable that there are a good number of neurotically-based, self-defeating reasons for extramarital affairs.

Varieties of Self-Deception:

EGO BOOSTING

An affair that is engaged in to avoid personal or marital problems, or to do something to a third party (such as an affair of revenge), or for ego bolstering (going from one relationship to another with the purpose of enhancing one's feelings of potency and power) is self-defeating. It is self-defeating in the same manner that heroin addiction is: it simply doesn't work in the long run. The relief is temporary, the problem remains unsolved, or indeed, is complicated by the attempted solution.

When Dan and Barbara first married, he thought, "She has

everything." She took away his anxiety in being with a woman, did most of the talking, brought home a terrific executive salary, and, by her social adeptness, determined their day-to-day activities. Initially, Dan felt some of Barbara's supercompetence would "rub off" on him. Instead, shortly after they were married, Dan felt that his inadequacies were highlighted by Barbara's attainments; he felt less brilliant than she, awkward with people in general, and frustrated by his inability to progress in his career as rapidly as his wife. Barbara, for her part, was content that Dan was responsible, considerate, and a loving father. She loved him and did not make the kinds of torturous comparisons that Dan did, and on several occasions she reassured him of this. Unfortunately, Dan would not accept what he viewed as a one-up/one-down relationship. He was sure that she and their entire social circle undervalued him and that sooner or later his wife would admit her unhappiness with his inferiority and run off with someone who was her equal. "Why would she want to continue living with me? Realistically, I don't measure up to her business associates; I just haven't made it."

Dan, in a futile effort to buffer himself from his wife's and their friends' "rejection," had a number of affairs with women who he knew couldn't measure up to him. He felt that because they had done poorly in life, they would think him rather terrific.

"I needed these affairs. I always felt I needed shoring up. The only thing I was ever sure of about myself was that I was good-looking. Nothing else. I had no confidence in myself as a person of intelligence. What intellectual veneer I had was polished onto me by Barbara. I don't even have confidence in myself as a lover. So I go thrashing about, always looking for reassurance."

Some of us, like Dan, are so perfectionist in the demands we place on ourselves and so self-demeaning when we do not live up to these demands that we cannot bear to face ourselves or our mates, who know us with all our inadequacies. We condemn ourselves for not being up to par as housekeepers, athletes, parents, lovers, or monetary providers.

Male-female roles being what they are in our society, husbands who are adulterous because of personal feelings of inadequacy frequently view themselves as incompetent because of professional or business failures and think they can somehow compensate for these defects by sexual conquests; while wives who are adulterous as a result of their feelings of worthlessness commonly believe they are boring, noncontributive, and sexually inferior, and that the affair will make them seem exciting and amorous.

The pattern is, first, to set up unrealistic demands that deprive us of our self-worth, and then to seek relief in affairs (or alcohol, drugs, or compulsive job hopping). The purpose is diversion and temporary relief from discomfort. The relief is merely palliative and ultimately self-defeating, for the problem exists in the person's head, in the insistence that in order to be an acceptable human being, to like yourself, you have to excel. This perfectionist, unrealistic demand is what needs rethinking; the screwing, drinking, and other compensatory behaviors only evade the real issue and may even make things worse. Sure, you may be comfortable while doing these things but the comfort is short-lasting and may be at the expense of personal and marital growth. The question is, what do you want? Temporary relief or the longer-lasting, life-promoting goal of working things out with yourself and your marriage?

AVOIDANCE

Just as extramarital sex was used by Dan to boost his sagging ego, it can be used to avoid psychological hangups. Rather than face and eventually work out marital, social, or work problems, the affair can be used as an easy out. It seems easier to run from affair to affair than to confront a drab, meaningless existence.

A case in point involves Carol, a very bright woman in her early thirties, who has been married for six years to an engineer. Carol had quit college after one semester because she found the work too demanding. She then dabbled for short periods in photography and painting. While she was doing well in these areas, she felt encouraged and enthusiastic. However, as soon as

things became more difficult, she gave up. The same pattern oc-
cured with tennis, an attempt to go back to school, music
lessons, and a host of other activities—short-lived enthusiasm,
then decline, and eventual termination of the activity. Each time,
when the activity became a bit too difficult, Carol's interest
began to wane. As a result of her attitude—"If things get hard I
won't be able to measure up, so I'd better give up"—Carol had
no vital absorbing interests in life. Because she refused to work at
finding major goals that would give more meaning to her life, she
rather easily fell into a series of affairs to forget the aimlessness of
her existence. As Carol explained:

"After two years and numerous affairs, I'm not any happier; if
anything, my life is even more of a mess. I've neglected my
children and my husband. I've acted in ways that I don't respect.
It's very difficult to acknowledge that I've been wasting my life.
As a child I can recall being told, 'Oh Carol, you're so bright,
you'll do well at whatever you try.' Like hell! Knowing that it
was expected of me made doing well an obsession. Even if I did
well, keeping it up put an enormous strain on me. I remember an
incident that occurred out west. I was training to be a race car
driver. Imagine, I was hoping to be the first competitive woman
driver. I was enrolled in a well-known school for professional
drivers. One day at the start of a practice race I heard that
several of the other drivers, instead of being amateurs, were real
pros who had stopped by to shape up. I became so frightened
that I just looked absolutely straight ahead. I glued my eyes to a
spot about five feet ahead of the car, and as we moved out at the
start of the race, I just maintained this concentrated stare directly in front of the car. Well, about midway through the race I
dared to look back and noticed I was way out ahead of the
field—pros and all! Immediately, I took the escape route off the
track. If I had won that race, could you imagine the expectations
people would have had for me next time out? I quit racing soon
after that.

"My affairs, as I see them now, were evasions. I blamed my
marriage; I blamed my robust sexuality. I realize now that I

wasn't merely seeking an adventurous relief from marital boredom or even feeling particularly lustful. Actually, my marriage had been quite satisfactory. I can't blame that. No, when I get right down to it, it's my personal problem that has led me to be so compulsively adulterous. I suppose it was a desperate attempt to fill up a life that I feel is shitted up. Except it didn't really work. Here I am two years later after lots of screwing, still screwed up. I still have no goals. I am still empty—except now I've jeopardized my marriage and I don't know if there's enough left to salvage."

As Carol herself recognized about her affairs—all with men who promised her everything but delivered nothing but heartache—she had gained practically nothing from these relationships but preoccupation. She had no constructive goal, she was merely filling up her time, and any long-range, organized purpose she might have developed was no nearer to fruition.

Another type of avoidance that frequently motivates extramarital sex is the refusal to acknowledge that one is growing older. It is no secret that our society is obsessed with youth. Youth has been made synonymous with beauty, vitality, gaiety, and idealism—all that is good, pure, and, especially, joyful. Age has become a specter to be feared and a process to be fought. This adulation of youth touches us all; we are exposed to it continually. Whether our youth has been joyous and carefree or not (and for most of us it was a difficult period), the distortions of time may cause us to remember it as one long "good time." If, on the other hand, we remember those adolescent years with pain and as a time of loneliness and rejection, we may long for a youth we feel we missed. Thus an exciting affair may be thought of as a means of living the carefree youth we missed or of reliving one that is more a fantasy than a memory.

Jerry, a man nearing his forties, was, as a teenager, very shy and generally inhibited, particularly with girls. He had terrible acne and always worried that girls would find him offensive. As he got older, his complexion cleared and he married Lisa, the first girl he dated. Jerry was twenty-four years old. Lisa was a calm, reserved woman who Jerry felt loved him very much.

Regarding his many affairs, Jerry, while studying his reflection in my office window, put it thus:

"I didn't want to have affairs. The last thing I'd want to do is to hurt Lisa. Yet I've felt compelled to see other women. I feel I've missed something in my life. I've lost my youth; I'll be forty next month! If it wasn't shyness, it was making ends meet—always something. Now I want to make up for lost time. The first time I had an affair was so exciting—secret meetings, great sex all afternoon, dangerous, mysterious—I felt like a young man again . . . alive. I don't want to be just another aging, weary commuter. It would be very painful for me to end up like my father, who, as far back as I can remember, was a dull, paunchy, TV addict who had just given up. That's not for me! Affairs are my youth connection. I need them to keep me alive, and I admit this type of renewal is very important to me."

Certain ages have taken on almost symbolic meaning in our society. Thirteen represents the threshold onto adolescence, twenty-one signifies the rights of adulthood, and age thirty for women and forty for men are given a significance that has no necessary relationship to reality. Overnight women see themselves turning old, losing their vitality, and, above all, their attractiveness. They spend hours searching for and worrying about wrinkles and compulsively try to offset the aging process so that their husbands will not lose interest in them.

For Jerry and for many men, age forty seems to carry the same significance, but with the added complication that they fear it marks the decline in their virility. The so-called roving forties is a reflection of this phenomenon. Some husbands, fearing a loss of sexual vitality with the onset of middle age, set out to "prove" they are still young lovers. Interestingly, various studies, including the reports of Kinsey and his associates, have shown that virility does not take a noticeable drop at age forty, but if a man *believes* his potency will drastically diminish then, it probably will, and his attempts to restore it through sexual affairs will probably be futile.

In a later conversation with Jerry, he said to me, "I was raised in a family where it was evident that after the first three decades of life, there was no joyful living. I was taught by my dad's example, and I foolishly believed that at middle age you might as well curl up and die. My affairs are largely an overreaction to that environment."

This is the crux of the compulsive drive to recapture a youth that never was—the belief that youth is the last opportunity to experience joy and excitement and that the later years of life and marriage are doomed to be routine, boring, and filled with long-dead dreams. It bears a psychological similarity to the strong fear of death so many of us experience; we fear we may die without ever having lived. Compulsive adultery is a very limited solution to this dilemma. How we choose to perceive our age will determine whether we dig an ever deeper rut while trying to relive our lost youth through sexual conquest, or whether we continually learn more ways to live our lives to the fullest with an insight not available to youth.

HOSTILITY

One of the more common self-defeating motives for an affair is revenge. Typically, one of the marital partners holds many hidden grudges against the other; he or she has a lot of unexpressed anger against the spouse. The anger may be denied; even the fact that a problem exists may be denied. The other partner is typically willing to show anger and does, and is manipulative in dealing with his or her "passive" mate. The withdrawal of the passively angry partner is a result of having no effective outlet for communicating his anger. He seems to be unable or unwilling to show his anger toward his mate either to place strong limits on what he will and will not tolerate or to clear the air between them.

Perhaps even more important than the lack of open, angry communication by the withdrawing mate is the absence of appropriate assertive behavior. He does not seem to be able to express his own likes, or his mate is able, by manipulation, to prevent him from acting on his own desires. The passive mate seems dreadfully lacking in the ability to tell his spouse calmly (or not so calmly) of his displeasure with the way things are going between them. Instead, the "silent" mate withdraws and fantasizes ways to "get back."

Roslyn, a very attractive, intense woman with a twelve-year-old daughter, has been married twice and has been adulterous in both her marriages. The first time she used extramarital sex mainly to find a man who would rescue her from a marriage that had deteriorated. Once married to a gynecologist, the man who had taken her out of her first unhappy marriage, she continued to use extramarital sex because, she said, her second husband took her for granted and put her very low on his list of priorities.

"Being a product of my times, I use extramarital sex as a weapon. My husband works long hours when he really doesn't have to, and I resent it. When he comes home, he is preoccupied. He wants to watch television, read, sleep, or go on his boat. That boat is driving me crazy. I don't want to compete with a goddam boat! I feel he would choose that boat over me without an instant of hesitation. I don't feel married. It seems he regards me as a convenience. When he is attentive, it is often in a belittling and critical manner; he makes me feel stupid and ridiculous. One time I was relining the shelves in one of the closets very meticulously because I like things to be perfect and beautiful, and he nagged me something awful and called me a fool for wasting my time on something no one would ever see. So, either he pesters me or he ignores me, and I don't have the courage to tell him I don't like him doing that, at least not with the rage I feel. I simply have lovers. And then, when my husband continues to ignore me, to take me for granted, or comes on with his criticisms, I sit back, smile inside, and say to myself, 'You're not so hot, you fool.' That's my revenge!"

Roslyn sought revenge for her husband's inattention. A somewhat different example of a hostility-motivated affair involves Mr. and Mrs. Herbert Blake, a prosperous suburban couple who have been married for fifteen years. They had two

teenaged children and were socially popular. Everybody thought
they had a fine marriage, Mr. Blake was an executive with a substantial income. His wife was well-dressed, played excellent
bridge, and did more than her share of local charity work. Both
were considered socially desirable, well-informed conver-
sationalists in their set, but at home Mr. Blake rarely said much.
To keep the peace, he went along with whatever his wife wanted.

One day shortly after leaving for an all-day charity event, Mrs.
Blake returned home unexpectedly for the raffle tickets left on
the kitchen table and discovered Herbert in bed with another
woman. At first, she was incredulous, then horrified. In the
marital crisis that followed, Mrs. Blake learned that the "silent
treatment" she had received all these years was not cooperation
or strength but hostility camouflaged by phony and misleading
compliance. Mr. Blake admitted that he had never leveled with
his wife, never clearly communicated his feelings about the way
she dominated most of the family decisions. Though it riled him
to no end when she decided what they should do to "have fun"
or to be creative," almost invariably he went along with her
ideas. On the few occasions when he did protest mildly—always
without making the true depth of his feelings clear—he found
that his wife became even more assertive. So he became quieter.
As he put it:

"I felt it undignified to get in there and really let her have it. I
grew up in a family with a lot of screaming. I remember the
hurts, the insults, the pain, and meanness very vividly. I didn't
want that in my life. I didn't want to get embroiled in the kind of
rage my parents expressed. Yet being dominated, bossed
around, feeling like a doormat, wasn't my cup of tea either. I
chose an affair—with a particularly passive woman, by the
way—as an equalizer. Taking her to the house, of course, was
stupid. Although if I'm going to be brutally honest, I must admit
to having mixed emotions about being caught, part of it being,
'Good, you bastard, at last you can unmistakenly see you are not
dealing with the village idiot!' I feel curiously relieved."

Both Roslyn and Herbert Blake share a common deceptive belief: It isn't "gentlemanly," it isn't "feminine," to express emotionally and firmly dissatisfaction and annoyance. It isn't nice. It isn't mature. This is supposed to be the age of reason, so we must always act civilized and reasonable. Only we don't always feel civilized and reasonable! Ideally, marital communication is best if conducted in a harmonious manner but this need not always be so. Shrieking and yelling, accusations and counteraccusations, nasty comments and snide retorts and other unpleasant ways of interacting are in many cases the best a beleaguered couple can do in the beginning.

Despite the fact that after the first few minutes brawls become counterproductive and make things worse, they can be very revealing and useful in their initial heat. "You don't love me anymore. You never put your hands on me except when you have sex on your mind. You never do anything to help me, but if Phyllis Taft wants a hand with her packages, that's a different story. You can go to hell as far as I'm concerned." This is a very important message that perhaps could only be delivered, at the time, in sobs and shouts. Indeed, any kind of communication that deals with what is wrong with an ailing marriage is likely to be better than no communication at all.

This does not mean that I advocate brawling. It merely means that many couples cannot begin to communicate in any other way, especially about the things that are really bothering them. Some beginning is better than none at all, especially if there is awareness of what is going on and if the bickering is viewed as a primary stage of communication that can develop into a more harmonious dialogue. An affair is not likely to help. It will merely give one person an unfair advantage over the other.

Affairs of resentment may also be a form of rebellion in a marriage that at base is solid. The rebellion in these cases is against married life, the grievance being that it forces one to give up the pleasures of the single life in return for the special fulfillment only marriage can provide. Carl is twenty-eight, he has been married for five years.

"When my wife was in her sixth month of pregnancy, it hit me—I'm stuck; I'm really married. We had been married for several years, but I never felt trapped, or as if I was really married. There were no real responsibilities. With a child coming, I felt really scared. Was I doing the right thing? Was marriage really for me? Up until then I had never really had to consider those questions. I guess in the back of my mind I always figured I could get out. With the pregnancy, I saw it as too late—what kind of heel would leave his wife in her sixth month? I couldn't live with that, but I also felt, for the first time, really tied down. What a lousy sense of timing. When Cathy flew to Minnesota to visit her aunt, I remember thinking maybe the plane will crash and I'll be freed. It was a horrible thought. I was ashamed that I could even think such a thing. Although I was doing a lot of bickering, I always considered Cathy a friend, a very decent, giving, and accommodating person. I was beside myself.

"My affairs—and there were many—made the statement, 'I won't be restrained by any societal rule,' and closer to the heart of the matter, 'Cathy, damnit, how could you do this to me? I'll show you that I can't be contained.' The whole thing was unreasonable. I failed to take responsibility for my own actions. I was into blaming. Paradoxically, when I realized the choice to adventure sexually or not was mine, that it was up to me to decide—when I really felt that, I no longer had any desire to stray. It wasn't sex all along; it was the severe proscription that I wouldn't accept."

UNSELECTIVE SELECTION

Unlike Carl, who had chosen a basically compatible mate but perhaps at too early an age, some individuals choose poorly. With them, it is not so much the affair itself that is unwise but the choice of the marital partner that elevates the affair to such status. Edith, a passionate, earthy woman already once divorced, explains her affairs as a matter of sexual deprivation:

"My honeymoon was a nightmare, an absolute, utter night-mare. He just seemed to disintegrate under the pressure of hav-ing to make love. Making love just didn't seem to be his forte. I really hated going to bed with him after a while and only did it because I felt ashamed just to masturbate, but actually being sexually involved with him was a turnoff. He'd touch me, get me all aroused, then enter and come one second later. When I just met him I figured that after we were married, he'd relax and get over it slowly. As it turned out, things got worse instead of better. A lot of the time, he couldn't even get it up. I had to have some relief or I thought I'd go out of my mind."

The point here is that Edith, who had had plenty of premarital experience and numerous affairs between marriages, should have known better. Sex is very important to her, yet she married a man who had sexual difficulties. She made this mistake because of her strong need for a passive and inadequate man she could take care of. Unfortunately, she found she was no Florence Nightingale. Eventually her husband discovered her affairs and left her.

In contrast to Edith are those who neither chose a mate neurotically nor deliberately create a frustrating situation, they simply choose marriage partners before they are experienced enough to know what they are doing, or they believe their part-ner's deficiencies aren't so serious that they will drive them to af-fairs for compensation.

For all these people—those who enter the world of ex-tramarital affairs as a short-sighted solution to emotional or marital difficulties—the affair is not a luxury, it is an absolute necessity as proof of personal power, vindictiveness, or reas-surance. Sensual pleasure is not what these people are seeking in each new conquest; rather they want to alleviate the pain in aspects of their lives or marriages that they find insufferable. Rather than repair or leave a seriously ailing marriage or work on their problems, they engage in affairs that typically are shallow, brief, and numerous to the point of compulsive promiscuity. The needs these affairs satisfy can be subsumed under the heading "self-indulgence." In addition, just as these individuals, because of their immaturity, acted unwisely in their choice of a marriage partner or even in choosing to marry at all, their lovers are often equally unsuitable.

This is not to say that when someone has an affair or even a series of affairs for unwise, self-deceptive reasons, it is always a frustrating counterproductive experience. That would be too simplistic. Some people begin with primarily neurotic motivation but then discover some very important things about themselves in the course of their infidelities. This happened to Roslyn, who initially sought revenge in her affairs.

"After seeking comfort in a score of affairs and finding it only very briefly in each, I finally entered therapy and slowly discovered that in both my marriages I had chosen a powerful and punishing man very much like my own father, and hence I had neither been able to fight back nor walk out on my own. After two years of therapy, I divorced, spent a stretch of time being single, and then was remarried—this time to a totally different type of man. Truthfully, my affairs were mostly a waste of time, but not completely. I feel that my experience with many men is what first sparked the realization that it was I—not the man— who was the problem. That's when I decided on therapy. I don't know if I would have come to the same point without the affairs—I could simply have become resigned to my miserable fate."

Varieties of Self-Conception:

PLURALIST SEXUAL DESIRES

Just as extramarital desires and actions can be exaggerated, compulsive, and self-deceptive, they can also be ordinary, normal, and even indices of growth. Generally, an affair that is not pathological is one engaged in for its own sake. The individual seeks primarily neither to hurt another person nor to compensate for felt inadequacy, and does not feel compelled to carry out or continue the behavior if it endangers a valued marital relationship.

Perhaps the most frequent cause of infidelity is the simple, natural, normal feeling of boredom—sexual, emotional, or both. By nature most of us are varietists, and marriage, particularly over an extended period of time, smothers our varietist inclinations. That this natural varietist tendency of human beings is well within the normal range of behaviors and is not necessarily indicative of emotional or sexual disturbance is attested to by many outstanding authorities. For example, animal studies reviewed by Kinsey and his associates revealed that male rats, monkeys, and bulls who had been observed to copulate repeatedly until they became exhausted and stopped when restricted to one partner, would, if new females were offered to them, become remarkably restored and begin copulating with the new partners with nearly all the energy and excitement they originally had. Kinsey, considering these experiments along with a review of the anthropological evidence, concluded that the varietist urge is part of the mammalian nerve heritage and man is also subject to this biological influence. The male human being would, nearly always, behave pluralistically were it not for social restraints.

As for the female, in *Sexual Behavior in the Human Female* Kinsey and his associates write, "We have already observed that the anatomy and physiology of sexual response and orgasm do not show differences between the sexes that might account for the differences in their sexual responses." They conclude that the female's somewhat weaker polygamous tendency is probably a matter of social conditioning rather than instinct.

Two outstanding and highly respected sex researchers, Drs. Clellan S. Ford and Frank A. Beach, provide evidence on this point: In a summary of the sexual patterns in 185 societies, they point out that wherever there is no double standard in sexual matters, and extramarital liaisons are tolerated, women are as eager and ready for variety as men.

The desire for novelty and variety is apparently inherent in most human beings; long-term exclusivity with a sexual-emotional companion is not an innate human need, but a culturally induced one. Since we are by nature varietists and by social/cultural upbringing exclusivists, we are frequently in conflict. And this is why many of us—even the normal and the satisfactorily married—are so sorely tempted and sometimes act on our desires for novelty and change. Sara, a suburban college instructor, age thirty-seven, mother of one, puts it this way:

"I love my husband very much. I love making love to him. I wouldn't want to live with anyone else. And I don't have to have an occasional affair. . . . Just as I'm sure I could live on a limited nutritious diet and stay healthy, I could live within the confines of my marriage and stay healthy. Admittedly, though, there is a degree of monotony that I see no reason to endure. I don't regard my very occasional affair as cheating anybody of anything. I am not taking inordinate time away from my family nor am I particularly preoccupied during these periods, which are infrequent and usually brief. My sporadic encounters may even contribute to the marriage. The liveliness and emotional satisfaction I derive definitely feeds back into the marriage in a positive way. As a matter of fact, it may be that during an affair I am more sexy and affectionate with my husband rather than less, as most people would think."

SEX/AFFECTION DEPRIVATION

Most of us have the security of sexual sameness and would like occasional variety. Some of us, though, do not have this security. That is, some husbands and wives are sexually deprived either temporarily or permanently. They may be separated because of lengthy business trips or other obligations; one mate may be in exceptionally poor health for an extended period; or one may have a substantially higher sex drive than the other. In these circumstances, the deprived mate may develop feelings of resentment that can easily disrupt a relationship that in most other aspects is quite satisfactory.

Lyle is an architect who has been married to Ginger for fourteen years. He is very successful in his field and has won several professional citations. He describes his marriage as "right out of the storybooks—we are both loving and considerate to each other." Lyle characterizes his wife as "a typical, home-loving soul, very family-oriented." They live in a suburb. He commutes each day while she gardens, refinishes antiques, and prepares gourmet meals. They have three children. Lyle described his affairs to me this way:

"I become involved in affairs as a supplement to my marriage. I simply have much more desire for intimacy and much more sexual energy than my wife could possibly absorb. To deny myself the affairs and to direct the resulting frustration at my wife might be more honest, but very cruel. My wife has an open attitude toward sex and would probably not be shattered if she found out about my affairs. Yet she prides herself on meeting most of my needs and would be hurt. I am especially careful about this. I seek out women who are, to some degree, unfulfilled at home, yet who are strongly committed to their families. They feel safe having an affair with me because of my commitment and I feel safe with them.

"One of the things I value most about extramarital relations is getting to know another person on an emotional level. Not that it is always intimate just because we have sex, or that it can't be if we don't, but there have been disclosures in some of my relationships that have contributed to me as a person. My wife, who overall I would choose over any of the other women I've known, does not have the instability, the outright craziness that some of these women possess.

"It seems that there are advantages and disadvantages to any life choice. I wanted a woman who was stable, not neurotically demanding, and, of course, loving. Ginger is all of these things. An occasional fling with someone like Jana, a Greenwich Village poetess with long black hair and electrifying eyes, is fantastic, though. She is nothing like Ginger. She does not want a family commitment, and living with her would be nothing short of a disaster, and Jana is wise enough to know that. Is she crazy? Not really, just not made to live with another person, but in bed she is like a volcano, erupting to the touch. I don't want to give that up unless it will interfere with my primary commitment to Ginger and the children."

DIMINISHMENT OF INNOCENCE

As the decision in favor of an affair may be for inappropriate or unwise reasons, so may the refusal of an affair. Many persons avoid an affair because they need to feel innocent or because they are extremely dependent on their spouses. These attitudes are appropriate to growing children and it seems many people fail to achieve adult autonomy. Those who are caught in this impasse may have an affair in order to perform as "bad child" or may refuse an affair in order to perform as "good child." In either case, their behavior is immature not because of the act or the refusal to act but because of the basis on which the decision is made.

The need to feel innocent, that is, remain the "good child," is a common phenomenon in our society. People have a need to feel innocent in direct proportion to their lack of maturity. The process of fulfilling one's sexual potential, because of the special meaning given to sex in our society, is a continuing story of the loss of innocence. Roberta, a woman of thirty-three, recalls her experiences in this regard:

"My relationship with my parents as a youngster was pretty good. They were sophisticated and highly-educated people who never really told me what to do, but there was a very strong emotional connection there and it was very important to me to please them. When I reached late adolescence and began to masturbate, I felt trusting of them and discussed it openly. I recall them being pleased by this. And, in turn, I was pleased by their acceptance. As I see it now, though, my confession was not merely an act of openness and trust, but a struggle to regain my lost innocence. In actuality, the discussion with my parents was aimed at getting their approval. I was not autonomous enough to come to terms about this by myself—or through my peers.

"My premarital sexual experiences had the same tone. They were, in important respects, similar to my adolescent struggles. I did not have intercourse previous to marriage but I did practically everything else. Again, I saw not "going all the way" as retaining my "goodness." One time, involved in very heavy petting, I became so sexually excited that I got scared and began to bawl. I cried because I felt driven to complete the act but yet wouldn't for fear I would lose something. This was about three months before I married and the man involved was my fiance!

"In my marriage, the principal deterrent to having an affair was the overriding need to feel innocent, to be a "good girl." To have an affair would be to lose that innocence. For one thing, I could not—that is, I would choose not to—be open about the affair. I could not share this aspect of my life with my husband. I thought about this and about the things that have occurred in the past with my sexuality. As a result, I decided to have an affair. It was brief and in itself not particularly terrific. My husband is a more considerate lover and a brighter, more exciting person than this other man—which I could have predicted because [my husband] Ron has so much going for him. But I regard the affair as a very important, positive growth experience. First, I no longer bear the burden of the necessity to be innocent. I guess I could have come to this same conclusion without the affair; I could have worked the whole thing out in my head, but it just didn't seem enough. It could too easily have been another rationalization to remain the 'good girl.' Second, I found that intimacy does not require complete disclosure of one's thoughts, feelings, and actions. Total openness is unrealistic. Each mature individual—and this is the point—carries with them some experiences that they need not share. I can now live with this comfortably. This type of privacy has no relation to shame. Actually, it is just the opposite; the compulsion 'to tell all' seems to me an effort to remove shame and guilt. The affair and its implications for me have been an affirmation; my independence, my autonomy as a human being, have been expanded. I prize that experience."

SEXUAL CURIOSITY

Closely related to a loss of innocence is sexual curiosity. Although an increasing number of people today have affairs between the time one marriage ends by divorce or death of a spouse and another begins, many mature adults (especially women) have had only one or two sex partners in their entire lives. Some of these people, both men and women, are shamed by this. They think to themselves, "What's the matter with me; in this enlightened age everyone should have varied sexual experiences." It is the shame that drives them to adultery. Others, including those who are happily married and who would never consider breaking up their homes, may be motivated not by the false dictum of "Thou Must Be Sexually Experienced" but by simple curiosity. Husbands and wives who engage in extramarital relations out of sexual curiosity may not constitute a high percentage, but those who consider it and are sometimes tempted to do it are legion.

Josephine married Eli when she was nineteen years old. They live in a small conservative community and have been married nine years. Their first child was born after two years of marriage, and the second a year later. For the past several years, Josephine has been too preoccupied with two preschool youngsters to give serious thought to her occasional sexual fantasies involving other men. Now that both children are in school, she finds herself more acutely aware of her sexual curiosity. Aside from teenage petting, Eli is the only man with whom she has had sexual experience. In my conversation with Josephine, she stated that although she is quite tempted to experiment with another man, Eli would be absolutely destroyed if he found out. "Realistically," she added, "in this community the chances of being caught are pretty high." Rather than take the chance and risk Eli's emotional upset, Josephine has decided, at least for the time being, to stay with her fantasies.

Josephine's desire, as she described it, did not seem self-deceptive. Nor would her acting on that desire be neurotic had her life circumstances been different. Her choice not to act appeared quite legitimate—that is, regardless of the legitimacy of her motives, her marriage probably would not have survived discovery and that was too heavy a price to pay. Perhaps most striking was her closing remark to me: "I do not feel cheated by my choice. I needn't satisfy my wants just because I would like to. I can stand not having it all."

Deciphering the Desire

Extramarital sexual encounters usually are multimotivated. That is, although we have been speaking of extramarital sexual behavior as though it were singularly motivated by a need to be assured or a need to impress or desire for closeness or for love or for variety, in reality it is usually a combination of these motives that propels an individual. Determining our motives, then, or the motives of an adulterous mate is no easy task. Indeed, to complicate matters, situational factors also influence an individual. For example, a relatively happy, emotionally stable man might never become unfaithful in a conservative community where the pressures to conform are strong. The same man, even if not particularly desirous of extramarital sex, might, if freed from external controls by a permissive community and a permissive wife, act upon his low-level urge.

So, how does one go about answering the question, "Why am I doing this?" or, in reflecting on the case of an adulterous mate, "Why did it happen?" First, it would be best to think in terms of primary motives rather than *the* motive. Additionally, a careful consideration of outside circumstances is helpful. These may range from the type of community one lives in to such things as career setbacks, life transitions (for example, the last child going off to school and leaving a housewife suddenly alone), and serious marital strife.

Honest, persistent questioning is probably the most useful

tack whether considering internal factors or external conditions. "Am I finding my marriage boring because I want to find it so in order to excuse my extramarital ventures? Am I trying to escape working at my marital relationship and making it more interesting? Is it really that my psychological hangups, economic problems, career difficulties, are bothering me, and the affair is a diversion from the painful task of solving these problems? Is my dissatisfaction with my marriage part of my general negative feeling about myself rather than a true reflection of my marital relationship? If I am feeling sexually deprived, have I given my mate the right of 'first refusal'—that is, what have I done recently to increase sexual pleasure with my spouse? Was it a persistent, honest effort? Am I actually that deprived sexually or am I using that as a rationalization to have a 'justified' affair? Do I merely want variety or am I insisting that I absolutely *need* it, *must* have it?"

An individual can ask himself questions like these, or a couple may engage in a dialogue based on these questions in an effort to determine what is wrong, if anything, and what a workable solution might be. Of course, an immediate, insightful answer will not always be forthcoming. An individual or a couple may well come up with few, if any, clear answers, or "answers" may be discovered that later prove to be false. Honest scrutiny of motives is not a foolproof course. It is impossible to be sure whether one's inquiries are logical or self-deceptive, or to predict with complete accuracy the effects of one's actions. But when your marriage, your well-being, or your spouse's well-being are at stake, this questioning process can be critical and instructive.

Discovery
An Emotional Crisis

Accidental Detection?

"I was going to a male psychologist at the time and I remember telling him I thought my husband was seeing other women. He kept asking me why I was so untrusting and insecure. He confused me and my husband confused me. Yet I was right after all. My instincts weren't wrong. I found out through my husband's diary that he *was* having affairs. He was also seen with her at a restaurant we frequently eat at. I was appalled. I begged him to stop. I carried on. I screamed, 'If you loved me, you wouldn't do this!' I ranted and raved and thought I was going to have a nervous breakdown. It took a long time for me to calm down. I felt like killing him, and at one point, I even got up to get a kitchen knife. I was frightened; frightened I might turn it on myself. During the course of the night, he made a clean breast of a whole lot of things he'd been doing over the past years; different women, women in his office, old friends of ours, business arrangements, and that sort of thing. He said none of it had been important to him; no one person. And he swore he'd change, give it all up. I believed him, it sounded as if he were honest. I assumed my crying and misery had had an impact on him.

"He was very apologetic and during the next year he kept bringing home gifts for me, and he was generally more thoughtful than he'd ever been. I was flattered, reassured, and I began to relax. Then there was this night when we were driving by his office after a movie, and he suggested we go up and screw on the rug. I found that very romantic. It was a Saturday night, the building was dark and empty; I felt as if this was a clandestine kind of thing and was very excited. I really got into a whole fantasy about it. After we made love and had gotten dressed, he went into the bathroom. He was taking a really long time, and I was sitting behind his desk waiting for him. After a while, I opened a drawer and staring me in the face was a letter that started out, 'To my lover.' Just then I heard him come out of the bathroom, and I grabbed the letter and put it in my pocket. When he came over to embrace me, I maneuvered around him saying I had to go now: 'It must have been something we ate.' In the bathroom, I read the letter. I was shocked.

"The letter was from a woman he worked with. It was a love letter. She described her feelings about an evening they had spent together the previous week. I remember that night. I wanted his companionship; I felt lonely. He told me he had a dinner date with a potentially important customer from out of town. 'It's one of those things,' he had said. The bastard! The letter mentioned me. This woman said she was jealous of me; she couldn't stand separating from him. She wanted him all for herself. She described some very private moments they shared. I felt as if someone had cut me open and pulled out my insides. Never have I felt so exposed, so vulnerable, betrayed. I trusted him; he had promised to stop a year ago when I was so distressed, but even then he wasn't honest. I threw up. After a while, I came out of the bathroom, and although I was shivering all night as if I were in shock, I didn't let on I knew anything."

When one partner discovers that a spouse is having an affair, the reaction is often profound shock followed by hurt, anger, and sometimes even guilt. It appears that sometimes the discovery is not purely accidental. The woman describing her experiences above detected infidelity twice. A diary kept, letters not destroyed, sometimes an indiscreet choice of meeting places—do these have a deliberate element?

Obviously, keeping extramarital sexual activities a total secret from one's mate takes some work. Besides the various possibilities of disclosure we saw earlier, there are innumerable others—an automobile accident; being seen by a friend; an injury to a child that causes a frightened wife to contact a husband who is not where he said he would be; a chance encounter with a relative; an unpredicted change in plans by a mate; pregnancy without marital intercourse; and venereal disease, which can be very difficult to explain if one's mate is afflicted. This is to say nothing of changes in attitude and behavior at home that arouse a mate's suspicions. In addition, there are telltale signs of extramarital sexual enthusiasm—smudged lipstick, unfamiliar perfume traces, bites, bruises, and scratches garnered in the heat of passion. Sometimes the evidence is deliberately planted by a lover to make trouble at home and force a separation.

Neither is it unknown for the affair-involved to summon a mate's attention by deliberately flaunting the affair—or at least a serious flirtation. Mental health practitioners are quite familiar with the husband or wife who is so careless with incriminating evidence that "accidental" detection is virtually inevitable. Such behavior may be a way of forcing the hand of a mate who refused to acknowledge that a marriage is in trouble. Detection may also serve the purpose of husbands or wives who want their mates to dissolve the marriage, thereby relieving them of guilt and enabling them to plead innocence (or at least "I should be forgiven") to children, relatives, and friends.

Thus, in an empty marriage, a mate may flaunt infidelity to provoke a spouse to divorce. Where the marriage is merely troubled, an affair may be a signal to the indifferent partner to pay more attention to the relationship. Of course, most people do not willingly acknowledge that the brazenness of their extramarital involvements conveys such purposes. Nor does the effect intended usually become the effect achieved. The husband who is indiscreetly conducting an affair to force his wife to pay more attention to him may find that she has been disgusted with the marriage for some time and this brazenness has merely provided the opportunity she has been waiting for to file for a divorce. Or a wife who is trying to provoke a husband into walking out on her may find herself trapped when her husband uses the detected affair as emotional and financial blackmail, threatens to leave her with nothing, and to reveal her to the children and her parents.

Occasionally, an individual will deny a mate's obvious extraneous sexual involvement because acknowledgment may be so threatening that it cannot be tolerated.

Arthur Fay, a large man with imposing stature, is a biologist in his early forties who specializes in cancer research. Fay is not the type of man easily forgotten. His direct, assertive manner leaves an impression on most people—they either appreciate him dearly or feel threatened and intimidated. His wife Beth also makes a notable impression. She is fair-skinned with shiny red hair, busty, and long-legged. Though not as gregarious as her husband, she makes up for it with her striking looks and quiet, keen intellect.

Mr. and Mrs. Fay sought professional help with their marriage for "communication difficulties." Frequently, this is a catchall statement that masks more specific dissatisfactions. In the sessions, it turned out that Mr. Fay wanted his wife to be more affectionate and sexual with him. Mrs. Fay wanted him to stop making so much of an issue about sex: "You know I am not a naturally affectionate person!" Mr. Fay complained frequently that his wife spent too much time away from home, and worse yet, as soon as she came in from an evening's volunteer work, would announce she had a headache, felt severely fatigued, or give some other excuse that would preclude sexual intimacy. Complaints, countercomplaints, and dissatisfaction were longstanding in the marriage. In the year before seeking professional intervention Mr. Fay felt particularly sexually deprived and resentful. Partway into their first therapy session together, the following dialogue took place:

Beth Fay: And another thing, you seem to resent my going out at night. The charity organizations I work for depend on me and that's important to me. All you worry about is how you can get in touch with me. I keep telling you I don't know which part of the hospital will be available for our meetings.

Therapist: Beth, you seem to be implying that your husband doesn't trust you. Is that so?

Beth Fay: (beginning to blush) Yes, either that or he is trying to control me and resents my independence.

Therapist: In what way might he not trust you?

Beth Fay: (neck and face crimson red) I don't know; you'll have to ask him.

Arthur Fay: (sitting stiffly and staring away from his wife's obvious emotional reaction to the therapist's probe) I'm not trying to control my wife; I would just like to see more of her.

At this point, the therapist did not pursue the possibility of affair involvement any further and at the end of the hour arranged to see Mrs. Fay the following week without her husband. After she was assured that confidentiality would be upheld, Mrs. Fay acknowledged an affair that had been going on for little over a year. Mr. Fay, a bright, scientifically trained, socially aware man, had come practically face to face with his wife's adultery, but he had blinded himself to the evidence. Probably a fair amount of middle- and upper-middle-class wives use the same strategy of denial Arthur Fay deployed. Dependent on their husbands for the creature comforts they've come to enjoy—vacations, country-club membership, designer clothes—they consciously or unconsciously refuse to see anything that would disrupt the marital arrangement.

True Confessions

There are times when an affair does not require accident or indiscretion to be discovered. On rare occasions, a suspicious spouse will hire a detective to gather definitive evidence. This tactic is usually employed at the urging of a lawyer, and even then with great reluctance because of its humiliating effects on both marital partners. More commonly, some adulterous people feel compelled to confess their sexual adventures to their mate. The motives behind voluntary confessions vary; guilt and the need to be forgiven are probably the most common. A typical pattern following an abrupt confession to one's spouse is that the one who confesses becomes the target of anger, hostility, and/or shame. He or she may then experience punishment, and as a result, feel cleansed and restored to innocence:

"I had this nagging guilt. My wife and I are close; we share things together and have a commitment to each other. My deception about the affair really bothered me. There were a number of underhanded things I noticed myself doing to ease my discomfort. For example, I would come home and be very critical—provoke fights, in fact. What I really wanted was for Joyce to say, 'You son of a bitch, go to hell!'—something that would relieve me of my responsibility. This way I could say to myself, 'Well, we're on the outs; the old rules are null and void.' The problem is that Joyce is so tolerant of me that it didn't work. I couldn't get her to give up on me. I also tried flirting in front of her, hoping that she would take the hint and give me permission, like, 'Okay, I can see you want to make it with another woman, go ahead, be my guest.' That didn't work either, she wasn't about to offer her best wishes—that tolerant she wasn't. After a while, being too damned honest and conscientious for my own good, I couldn't keep things secret from her.

"It happened like this: We were at a party and Susan Fields was there. I said to my wife, 'I want to leave, let's get out of here; there is something I have to talk to you about.' She said, 'What's wrong?' and I told her that we'd discuss it on the way home. As we drove away from the party, I told her about my affair with Susan. It was a mistake; I knew it as soon as I started because her face flushed in a real scary sort of way, but it was too late. Her voice cracked as she asked me a lot of questions. Then she sort of curled up within herself and suffered in silence. If she had fought me, it might have turned me against her, and I could deal with that. But she was so hurt and so deeply unhappy, I couldn't handle it. Neither could she. We survived, but it left quite a scar on both of us."

When suspicion and mistrust arising out of extramarital involvement are a serious barrier to intimacy and the deceived spouse continues to probe the issue, a frank discussion, preferably with the assistance of a therapist, may improve the marriage. Of course, even at this juncture some people may choose not to be candid. A person remaining with a spouse for expediency's sake—for instance, a mother with several children who stays with her husband because she has no hope of employment, and who wants nothing from the marriage except financial support—may continue to lie in an effort to maintain the relationship. But those who wish to improve their marriage and foster mutual growth and trust would best consider honesty.

In cases such as the one detailed above, where there is little or no suspicion on the part of the mate, there is a good chance "enlightenment" will serve no constructive purpose and may well be severely disturbing to the unsuspecting. As a consequence, the confessor not only doesn't experience the return to innocence he sought, but frequently feels more like a heel. Further, the need to confess more often than not is a self-serving act to relieve guilt cloaked in a rationalization to renegotiate or remodel the marriage contract. Confirmatory views of the lack of wisdom of this type of behavior are found among the leading professionals specializing in the marital relationship. Carlfred B.

Broderick, director of the marriage and family counselor training program at the University of Southern California, offers his opinion in the journal *Medical Aspects of Human Sexuality:*

> Like any other remedy, confession of extramarital affairs to a spouse is only helpful under certain conditions. I have cases where such a confession set marital therapy back several weeks and at least two instances where it disrupted the marriage completely. Indeed, the potential for damage is so real that I have become a conservative on this issue. . . . There is no simple rule of thumb that can govern all cases, but experience indicates that a conservative attitude toward confession is well justified.

Dr. Harold Winn, clinical professor of psychiatry at Temple University Medical Center, writing in the same journal, asks the question: "Should a husband or wife confess infidelity?" and answers: "In general, the response to this question is No." Dr. Winn points out that confessions of this sort may possibly relieve the guilt of the adulterer, but frequently will not be taken well by the other partner, and may actually be an act of conscious or unconscious hostility toward this partner. Also writing in the same journal, Dr. Charles E. Llewellyn, professor of psychiatry at Duke University Medical Center, adds his view:

> Should a husband or wife confess infidelity? An informal poll of friends, secretaries, colleagues, and students yielded a unanimous "No," but many elaborated their answers in some form. I agree with the general statement, "No.". . . In my opinion a husband or wife should not confess infidelity to the other unless he or she feels it necessary. I recommend that the involved partner discuss the situation with someone who is qualified to understand and work with the complexities of the situation and its meaning to the potential confessor, to the spouse, and to the marriage.

Even a high-ranking clergyman agreed. Bishop James Pike wrote that when two lovers have decided an affair is justifiable, they may have an obligation to lie about it for the good of the others: "Once a primary ethical decision has been made a particular way, more often than not secondary ethical responsibilities (i.e. secrecy and deception) are entailed."

Is all this to say that honesty between husband and wife had best be thrown to the wind? No, this is not the point. It is simply that most of us, in response to, "Did you have a nice day, dear?" are not ready for, "Oh yes, I spent the morning at a business meeting and spent the afternoon with a terrific lover, screwing to my heart's content. And how was your day, dear . . . ?" When a mate is unsuspecting, discretion, consideration, tact, and courteous selectivity are suggested.

Following this suggestion leads to one of the limitations of an affair: the joy of it does not lend itself to sharing with one's spouse. This is a limitation, but unless the affair is so time-consuming or suspicion-generating that cover-up lying becomes the rule rather than the exception, it does not necessarily limit marital intimacy. Real intimacy does not mean full disclosure of one's thoughts, feelings, and actions. Real intimacy is experienced only when people have the capacity and wisdom to give and to withhold, to move toward and to move away from, to be close and to be distant. In the great majority of marriages, total openness and closeness are oppressive and smothering goals. When the issue is extramarital sex, a "true confession" in the spirit of full disclosure is especially likely to produce panic and pain rather than permanence and peace.

Panic and Pain

The desire to be special to someone, to be "number one," to be wanted above all others, probably burns in all of us. No matter that this is an unrealistic ideal; the ground rules of traditional marriage attempt to secure it by emphasizing sexual exclusivity. The conventional clandestine affair to most of us constitutes a breach of trust, a violation of the implicitly agreed upon rules. When the deception is discovered, emotions ranging from panic to furious rage frequently result. Behavior varies from passivity (or perhaps more accurately, immobility) to violence. True, there may be people who are so secure that they are not particularly threatened by the discovery of their spouse's affair and who react with tolerance, understanding, and calmness. But, as Gracie Allen used to say, "There are a lot of people like that, but not many." Even those who have been having secret liaisons of their own react with deep shock, anger, and jealousy when they discover that their partner has been doing the same. Some people, so hurt by the experience, will view it as unforgivable and will move to break up the marriage. Others will see it as a symptom of what has been lacking in their marriage and will set out to do something about it. Still others will view it as not symptomatic of anything in particular and work toward a mutual agreement about such behavior. And there are those who will "stick it out" for reasons of economics, insecurity, children, or whatever, but will have only the coldest relationship.

Sometimes the discovery of an affair merely heightens a conflict that has been developing because of the emotion and time being drawn from the marriage. This is most likely to occur if either the affair or the marriage is highly involved. Of course, it is possible that more, rather than less, emotion will flow into the marriage as a result of an affair, but unfortunately, the effect is more often one of deprivation and conflict.

Where the extraneous sexual involvement is casual, the effect on the marriage may be very small until the affair is discovered. Then it is primarily the knowledge of the affair rather than the affair per se that is disruptive. A standard line of dialogue in Hollywood movies and novels used to involve a husband or wife discovering that the spouse has been unfaithful. "I suppose you'll want a divorce," one of them says, implying that divorce is the inevitable outcome of detected infidelity. This is indeed true in some marriages, but divorce is rarely sought because of infidelity alone. An affair that is dramatically discovered may be the final indignity that shatters a corrupt marriage, but when two persons have gotten along together reasonably well, one episode of infidelity will rarely trigger a divorce action. It may produce shock and resentment, and sometimes even physical estrangement, but not a sudden divorce. When adultery's ultimate impact on a marriage is divorce, it is usually the last straw in a slow, prolonged process of deterioration.

Coping: Destructive Tactics

The ultimate effect of a discovered affair depends also on the affair-involved individual's motivation—whether this is primarily "want"- or "need"-oriented—and, critically, on the spouse's interpretation of what the affair means.

"My spouse is having extramarital relations because he does not love me anymore and cannot bear to have me around him because I am stupid, boring, annoying, insensitive, and incompetent. Furthermore, I am sexually inadequate. This relationship is going to end our marriage. What will others think if they find out about our problems?" Obviously, husbands or wives who believe that an affair means their spouse no longer loves them, or that it is indicative of their own worthlessness, will feel and act differently from those who do not conclude from the experience that they are inadequate and their marriage is hopeless.

Most of us have inflated sexual behavior to unrealistic proportions. For one thing, we equate sex with intimacy. This is true sometimes, but certainly not always; sex is frequently not intimate, and intimacy often does not include sex. Moreover, infidelity, loosely defined as a breach of trust, may occur in many nonsexual aspects of a relationship but it is primarily the sexual that distresses us.

This leads to some interesting reactions; a person may be destroyed by a spouse's extraneous sexuality, even if assured it was casual and nonintimate, but relatively unconcerned by a mate's involvement with another in an intimate nonsexual exchange that is guaranteed to stay nonsexual. The point here is that extraneous sexual involvement, like all behavior, is open to many interpretations and the particular interpretation chosen is crucial to the feelings that are generated. Similarly, a man or woman who becomes distraught on learning of a mate's affair has several choices in expressing that feeling. She can, for example, proceed to suffer in grand and glorious style, all the while hoping that her mate will notice her pain and prove his love by rejecting the outside relationship:

Mate One: (letting her lip tremble just so) If you don't stop running around, we might as well get a divorce.

Mate Two: (in frustrated anger) Don't be silly. You don't really want a divorce!

Mate One: I do! Don't you care about our marriage and what I'll have to go through being single again?

Mate Two: (feeling guilty) Of course I care! What kind of a person do you think I am? I do a lot of things for you!

Mate One: You're selfish. You only do things that *you* care about. If you really cared about our marriage, you wouldn't have Sally Andrews on your mind. It's all your fault that I'm eating too much and getting fat. I do it out of the frustration you cause. You're going to drive me to suicide!

This approach is characteristic of the wronged mate who is passive and timid. The hurt is turned inward and is expressed in the form of accident, neglect of health, suicide attempts, and other self-destructive behavior. In the type of communication just illustrated, emotional distress is used as a tool to manipulate the involved mate. The object here is not direct and honest expression of authentic feelings; it is to induce guilt in the involved spouse and thereby control his behavior. The message is: "Stop what you are doing or I shall be even more miserable." This attempt to control a partner through guilt is often accompanied by an appeal to duty: "You owe it to me to stop seeing her." The pairing of a self-pitying moralist such as this and a guilt-prone adulterer provides an ideal setup for a destructive interaction. The moralist can play prosecutor, judge, and jury on one occasion, and then, in his additional role as victim, feel rejected, castrated, and sorry for himself—all the while provoking a guilty squirm or a flurry of angry self-defense from the affair-involved spouse. But this ploy has its disadvantages. As Bertrand Russell has written, "In former days parents ruined their relations with children by preaching love as a duty; husbands and wives still too often ruin their relations to each other by the same mistake. Love cannot be a duty because it is not subject to the will."

Replaying the guilt/obligation/duty message often enough frequently does exert a strong influence. Even if the unfaithful spouse is a low-guilt type, it plays upon his dislike of disruption at home and fear of being disgraced if his indiscretions become publicized. The impact is so potent that it sometimes terminates the marriage along with the affair.

"My wife and I had what I could call a guarded relationship. There were several touchy areas that we both avoided. When she found out about my other involvements, she initially used an appeal to sympathy (tears, outcries, visible suffering); then she resorted to what she called 'a reduction of services' (cold dinners, uncooperativeness, and the like); and then the final blow, an overdose of sleeping pills. One night, I came home late from a business meeting (I had stopped seeing other women months before) and she was lying unconscious in the middle of the living-room floor. There was an empty bottle of sleeping pills nearby where I couldn't miss them. I called the police and we took her to the emergency room where her stomach was pumped. She stayed overnight at the hospital and was released the following afternoon. That was it. The last straw. I couldn't take it any-more. I felt like a complete heel all over again. Suppose I hadn't come home when I did and she had succeeded? How could I live

with that? How could I leave the house every day not knowing
what she would do? I was frantic. How could I face anyone who
found out what this was all about? For the first time in months, I
started to consider leaving again. I just couldn't take the pressure anymore."

Occasionally, a spouse whose mate is unfaithful will make a
desperate effort to "get his act together." A man may lose
weight, become more discerning about his dress and general
appearance, and be extremely attentive to his wife in an effort to
compete with the third party. Following the suggestions of many
women's magazines, a woman will make a concerted effort to be
seductive, sexy, and passionate. But anger, hurt, and jealousy
are hardly conducive to such behavior and frequently it backfires.

Dori and Alvin are in their early forties. Two weeks before
Dori discovered that Alvin was having an affair, and since then,
despite his discontinuance of the affair, she has been trying to
deny her distress. Her attempts to play up to Alvin are both an
effort to keep him and a distraction from her emotional pain.
They have just finished having intercourse. She has pretended
passion, but she is not a good actress:

> Alvin: You don't seem to be getting much out
> of this anymore.
>
> Dori: Oh no, I enjoy it.
>
> Alvin: You don't seem to enjoy it like you used
> to.
>
> Dori: (her bitterness getting the best of her)
> You're not like you used to be.
>
> Alvin: (feeling angry) What the hell does that
> mean?
>
> Dori: Oh, Alvin, forget it. In a while, things
> will be better again. Let's give it some
> time.

Alvin: (his guilt and anger rising) I suppose you're referring to that thing with Florence Jackson.

Dori: I don't want to talk about that!

Alvin: Look, these things happen. Nobody's perfect!

Dori: All right, then, I'm not perfect either. Let's forget it.

Alvin: Forget it, my ass. You won't let me forget, that's clear from the cold shoulder you've been giving me in bed.

Dori: I never turn you down.

Alvin: But you never turn me on either. You go through the motions, but it's empty.

Dori: Alvin, don't push me. I'm doing all I can.

Alvin: (still feeling provoked and guilty) Do you think I like making love to a woman who's cold? This must be your way of getting back!

Dori: I'm not getting back at you. I'm trying to forget it! It's just that I have trouble feeling the same way I used to. Maybe in time it will get better. Time heals all wounds.

Alvin: If you want to call it quits, just let me know.

Dori: (her suppressed anger surfacing) So you can get back together with your girl-friend!

Alvin: Oh, for cryin' out loud, I've told you. . . . .

And so on. This kind of communication barely scratches the surface. The important feelings, underlying attitudes, and concerns go untouched. If denial and avoidance were not so prominant, this couple might have taken the opportunity to examine their feelings and attitudes toward each other, the circumstances and causes of the affair, whether it was a single chance occurrence or whether it reflects feelings that make the continuance of the marriage undesirable.

Sometimes a hurt, distressed mate tries retaliation. If John develops a sexual involvement with Helen, a friend of his wife Mary, then Mary may begin to go to bed with all of John's friends, and after doing so, throw it in his face. The result of this contest to see who can have the most extramarital sex and hurt the other most brutally is usually an empty marriage and empty sex.

"I was so hurt and angered by the discovery of my husband's affair that I did nothing for four days but cry. My face was puffy and raw. I couldn't hold food; my weight fell well below normal. After those initial days—I refer to them now as days of mourning—I started to plot and scheme. I tried to think of the best way of getting back. Howard has a brother. He is two years younger; he and Howard have been competitive all their lives. I know his brother finds me attractive. He's even made passes at me. I decided to seduce him. It worked without a hitch; his brother was most cooperative. Of course, when Howard found out (which I knew he would), he felt as if someone had driven a truck through his stomach. He came home infuriated, but he managed to keep his cool. I immediately knew what was up and I walked into our older daughter's bedroom with her and closed the door. He came charging in and said to her, 'Do you know what your mother did?' She replied, 'Yes, she told me, and I'm glad because you're a son of a bitch, and if that made her feel better, you deserve it!' That did it. He exploded; he was enraged. He pulled one of the wooden posts right off her bed and began smashing things. The room looked as if a bomb had exploded in it. I ran to call the police and he ripped the phone off the wall. He went insane. It was only then that I could feel compassion."

Sometimes the previously faithful partner may not flaunt the newly anointed affair in his mate's face. Merely knowing that "justice is being served" brings temporary relief. In other cases, the avenger subtly humiliates his spouse by conducting his illicit sex in such a way that the mate's friends and work associates know and the mate finds out through them. This is what occurred in the instance described above. Still others disclose their retaliation by evidence left about the house or scream it out in dramatic and frequently violent scenes. None of these actions is productive; sometimes they even have tragic consequences. One man who had been extramaritally involved, when confronted with his wife's retaliation, committed suicide. In another case, a young secretary, who little suspected that she was merely a weapon in a marital war, killed herself when the affair was abruptly terminated.

Coping: Constructive Tactics

The least popular but most constructive method of coping with the heightened emotions regarding the discovery of an affair is to face it squarely and openly discuss the feelings and implications involved. In the dialogue below, Dori and Alvin are beginning to communicate about his extramarital affair:

> Alvin: Dori, I am really bothered about the strain between us.
>
> Dori: Did I start it?
>
> Alvin: Drop that for a minute. The point is we're both unhappy, and if we just continue to drag on with blaming and counterblaming, it will end up in a divorce. If that happens, there's no guarantee that either of us will be better off. A lot of men are worse than I am, and I still prefer you to any woman I know.

Dori: Thanks. I'll tell Florence Jackson that the next time I see her.

Alvin: (not being sucked into a destructive argument) We have two children to consider. Their lives are also at stake here.

Dori: Does that scare you?

Alvin: Yes, it does. I am concerned that we work this out for them as well as for ourselves. I want to tell you how I feel about what has happened. We really haven't talked about it yet, just around it.

Dori: A little psychology lecture coming up?

Alvin: Maybe. Anyway, Dori, I feel very badly about what happened. I know you've been hurt and you're angry. I understand that. I want you to know that Florence really didn't mean that much to me; you've got it over her by a mile.

Dori: Oh, so you've come back to me on a rebound. Things didn't work out too well with Florence, is that it?

Alvin: No. Things could have worked out, but I didn't want to split. I want to be with you.

Dori: Well, I guess that's a compliment, in a backhand sort of way.

Alvin: On top of feeling guilty about all that's happened, I get defensive every time the issue comes up; I even feel tense in anticipation of it coming up. I get mad and accuse you of a lot of things that are really petty; spreading the blame around a little, I guess.

Dori: Are you apologizing? (Dori is beginning to change her reaction from sarcasm to sympathy in response to Alvin's persistent, honest, nondefensive stance.)

Alvin: I guess so. You know, I think, that this is difficult for me.

Dori: Yes, I do. Thanks.

Alvin: Your bitterness and bitchy attitude since you found out haven't made things any easier. It's hard to discuss your feelings if every time you open your mouth, you get walloped. (Alvin is beginning to define the issues blocking their communication.)

Dori: (nondefensively) How would you feel in my place? I felt humiliated and scared. Florence is five years younger than me; I felt as if I were being discarded for a newer model. I have felt old and ugly. Up to then I felt secure in our relationship. (For the first time, Dori is revealing very personal, painful feelings directly.)

Alvin: (softly, compassionately) Why did you try to hide those feelings from me?

Dori: I felt so vulnerable; I was protecting myself. I didn't feel safe with you. I still don't trust you as before. I know you've been trying to reach me; I agree that my attitude has made it harder.

Alvin: I understand more now of what's been going on inside of you, Dori.

In this dialogue, as contrasted with their earlier one, Alvin and Dori are less defensive and intent on avoiding honest expression. They are beginning to explore openly and honestly feelings about each other and about Alvin's affair. This is very difficult for Dori, who initially was sarcastic and defensive. Several times Alvin could have been pulled into an angry, counterproductive argument. Rather than expressing her feelings and wants direct-ly, Dori began by being hostile through her sarcasm. Attempts to lower the dignity and self-respect of a mate where there is intense anger and hurt are frequent, but it is self-defeating for the hurt person to hide his feelings and grin and bear it or to use them as a manipulative tool against the other.

There is a world of difference between a partner who openly states, "Hey, I'm hurting. Let's work this out," and one who demands, "You selfish bastard, you're hurting me. You have to stop! The latter's blaming and demanding attitude leads to counterattacks and the failure to achieve satisfactory commun-ication. Each conversation ends in a disruption; there is a lack of honest expression of feelings. Trust is not restored by these bouts and the fighting is likely to continue until the marriage is torn apart or has seriously deteriorated. Since these encounters are so sensitive, the communication is likely to be nonproductive unless one partner is able to stick to the problem at hand—that is, the hurt feelings, misunderstandings, and anger—as Alvin did (". . . the point is we're both unhappy"), even in the midst of blame-oriented messages ("Did I start it?"), such as Dori began with. Being understanding of Dori's feelings as well as honest about his own, and forgoing the temptation to counterattack, Alvin was able to create an atmosphere where Dori felt safe enough to ex-press herself honestly. This is a beginning.

Once emotions are directed toward the honest expression of feelings, it is important to examine what happened and its im-plications. What responsibility did each have for the affair? Was the affair part of a larger pattern of distrust and deception in the marriage? Are there things that can be done differently and more effectively in the marriage? What are the hopes and expectations for the future? Very specifically, what kinds of behavior are acceptable and what kinds out of bounds? Some couples may wish to renegotiate and remodel their marital agreement without restricting themselves to traditional sex-role expectations and definitions of fidelity. Others may resolve upon conventional standards. Still others may differ bitterly and require professional intervention.

Other important areas of discussion include sexual satisfactions, the type of affair, and its meaning. If the sexual relationship in marriage isn't satisfactory, how can it be improved? Was the casual affair engaged in because one partner felt the desire for sexual variety? What did the affair mean to the involved mate? He may say, "This was just a one-night stand. I don't love that woman; I love you." Then she may say, "Okay, I believe you." In these instances, trust and security may be restored by such simple measures as frequent reassurances of being loved and wanted, more frequent physical contact, cuddling and fondling.

If it was a high-involvement affair, the noninvolved mate has a right to know where he or she stands and rarely can be reassured quickly or easily. A shattered emotional investment of five, ten, twenty, or more years' duration is not easily repaired. It may be months or years before trust and a sense of security are reestablished. The marriage may never be the same. It is not unusual for the aggrieved spouse secretly to open up a separate bank account and take other actions to be financially protected in case of a recurrence or the dissolution of the marriage. This protective behavior may continue despite what looks like a healing of wounds on the surface.

One warning: Sometimes discussion of touchy issues can disrupt a relationship further by reopening old wounds and heightening distress to intolerable levels. If this occurs, it is time to work with a person in one of the psychological professions. Therapy may help pace interaction at a manageable rate and guide it along constructive lines. Even therapy, however, will only work if both mates want it, if both will start to listen as well as talk, and if both husband and wife will confront therapy issues openly rather than retreat into wounded silence or endless angry eruptions.

When an adulterous mate acts to restore the marriage and the spouse continues to grieve for a long time, there may be more basic reasons for the feelings of abandonment and rejection than are apparent. He or she may be reacting to childhood hurts—such as a father who neglected his family for his work, or a mother who had no time to show love for her children or was abandoned by a husband—or an old adolescent wound may have been reopened, and the distressed spouse may be reacting as he did when his girlfriend coolly cast him aside for a star athlete. These kinds of feelings, if persistent, are often characteristic of an individual who has not developed a sense of himself and of his own value. A developmental task of childhood involves moving beyond dependency on the parent. The same process must be repeated in the intimate partnerships of adulthood. If it is not, the discovery of an affair will be followed by unbearable and unceasing distress. In these instances, therapy is indicated. The best antidote to persistent distress is growth toward autonomy and self-direction. This kind of personal strength can make a person more attractive to his or her partner and less susceptible to feelings of insecurity, depression, and anger. A discovered adultery does not have to be a disaster; it is an experience that, like practically all emotional experiences, presents an opportunity for movement toward maturity.

Positive Effects

Against the Odds

Extramarital sex in our society is fraught with difficulties, dangers, and risks. The time commitment, emotional investment, deception, and lying, as well as the decreased attention and affection to one's spouse that may occur, frequently lead to several negative effects. These include: (1) an erosion of communication, trust, and security; (2) the stimulation of destructive jealousy and the heightening of feelings of inadequacy; and (3) the rapid and agonizing deterioration of a shaky and only intermittently satisfactory marriage should the affair be discovered. Even solid, well-functioning marriages are likely to be adversely affected by an outside amorous involvement. The damage may be sharp and sudden when provoked by discovery, or slow and subtle when the affair is undiscovered but long-term. Aside from being detrimental to the emotional well-being of one's mate and family, affairs conflict with middle-class mores and can be professionally and socially hazardous. The instances in which extramarital sex is handled carelessly and neurotically

are legion. The results are messy, emotionally painful, and disruptive. Broken families and broken people are not an uncommon consequence.

The Judeo-Christian tradition, which has always been critical
of the enticements and rewards of adultery, deems the act
nothing more than an indulgence of animalistic instinct by people who are emotionally weak and spiritually empty. This is one
view of adultery.

The other part of the story is that extramarital sex can have
positive effects on maturity, personal growth, and the marriage.
Both responsible and irresponsible, well-coupled and poorly-
coupled, happy and unhappy people are sexually monogamous.
The same applies to the nonmonogamous. Many less than ideal
marriages, those that are borderline or unstable, manage to survive and benefit the participants. The same applies to extramarital arrangements.

Julia, a thirty-three-year-old high school English teacher, has
been married six years and has a three-year-old son. Her husband, Bruce, is an architect. Julia has a warm, pleasant face and
her eyes sparkle as she talks about her affair.

"I have known Fred for four years; his wife and I work together. During the times we have been together, at parties,
school functions, and so on, Fred would usually flirt with me.
Since I noticed that he flirted with many of the other women, I
never thought much of it. Then two years ago he started to call
me and ask me out. He's a salesman and arranges his own hours.
At this point, I still didn't take him seriously—or didn't want
to—and jokingly put him off. I would say things like, 'You must
have the wrong number' or 'What's a nice guy like you . . .?'
When I look back, the way I denied my feelings about those initial flirtations, and later, the more direct invitations, was so
typical of me. My feelings so often get buried under words. It's
an occupational hazard. I still have a strong tendency to talk
about my feelings rather than experiencing them—but less so
now. Fred persisted and eventually I relented. Strange how it
happened. I called him. One day I was in his neighborhood—
with no real reason to be there—and I decided to see if he was

home. He was, and we met in a bar. From the moment we sat facing each other alone, on a cloudy, gloomy afternoon in that bar, it felt good to me. It felt right. We drank and we talked, and talked and drank, until we were both very high and had told each other an awful lot about ourselves. That's how we spent the first afternoon together. The next time we met, a week later in the early evening, we were both starving so we drove over to a delightful out-of-the-way restaurant and picked up right where we left off—talking. We talked all the way through dinner and into the evening. He told me about his marriage and I told him about mine. He gave me the idea that his wasn't the greatest and he stayed away evenings for that reason, but he didn't pretend for a minute that he was considering divorce.

"We continued to meet and talk. First there was a good-night kiss, then petting. After about three months, we had intercourse. Our sexual relationship was fantastic. I had never been as sexually excited and responsive as I was with Fred. But this wasn't the important thing; most important to me was the whole way I felt about myself when I was with Fred. This is when I first became aware of how distant I am from my feelings. Fred confronted me constantly. In a compassionate and loving way, he prodded me to express my feelings, to act on them, to be alive! We did such outrageous things together, I was really beginning to be less controlled; I was trusting myself more, trusting my instincts. I realized then that Bruce, as sweet as he is, is also out of touch with his feelings. We were both on a treadmill racing to keep up with the Joneses, the American dream—big house, two cars, prestige, achievement, everything that, in the final analysis, is of no consequence. I panicked when I first realized that. 'Would I be able to continue with my marriage now? Would it be too stifling? Could Bruce also grow or had I outgrown him?' These questions plagued me. I didn't want to break up my marriage, but what I was experiencing was too important to ignore. I had done enough of that! It is very difficult to be reborn, and I didn't want to return to the deadness. This is where the panic came in. I knew there was no returning. I wouldn't allow myself to vegetate as I had been doing all my life—at any cost.

Either Bruce came along on the trip or I was determined to take it alone. It occurred to me that Bruce could also benefit from an affair. I fantasized some woman opening his eyes to life the way Fred had done for me. This could potentially enrich our relationship, but I never pursued it beyond fantasy. It was too risky, and I didn't have the guts to suggest it.

"My first impulse with Bruce was to be resentful, critical, and arrogant. I wanted to show him quickly how much more there was to life. I wanted immediate results. I felt like saying, 'Look at me, I know where it's at; you're asleep.' I wanted to shout and scream when he denied his feelings and continued to plug along in the rut we were in. For a while, I did all of these things. I ranted, raved, bragged, cajoled, pouted, sulked, acted impulsively, etc., etc. In response, I got strain, anger, and tightness. More and more of what I didn't want. When things were at an all-time low, I called a very good friend of mine in Maine. I explained to her what had happened between Fred and me and what was happening to my marriage. Her response was simple. 'Let me see if I understand what you're saying, Julia,' she began. 'You've grown and expanded yourself through a loving and compassionate relationship. Now you are demanding that Bruce fit your image of an aware, adventurous, exciting, perceptive man. And you'd like him to meet your demand immediately and under duress. Is that it?' Well, I got the point. That was a year ago. After that conversation, I came down to earth. I began to respond positively when Bruce acted in a way I desired. I cut out the criticism. I prodded, but gently. I tried to provide the kind of nurturing Fred had provided for me. . . . Last night we had one of our best evenings ever—it was really marvelous—and afterward, as we lay in bed having a cigarette and feeling very affectionate, Bruce began to talk about his feelings toward his father, about what his son meant to him, and about what he felt toward me. We talked, embraced, and cried in each other's arms until early morning. As far as I'm concerned, this was the first time we had made contact since we met nine years ago. You asked if my marriage was helped by an affair. The answer is no. Helped isn't strong enough. It was saved!"

Research, Informed Opinion, Etc.

Is Julia's description of the extraordinarily positive effect of her extramarital experience on her own growth and her marriage to be trusted? There is no reason to consider her experience less valid than those extramarital experiences that contribute to unproductive strain in a marriage. Of course, conclusions such as Julia's will draw many detractors. The late Dr. Abraham Stone would probably have been among them. Dr. Stone, a distinguished pioneer in family planning and marriage counseling, stated in an article published in *Readers Digest* in 1954, "From my quarter-century of counseling on marital problems, I cannot recall a single case where infidelity has strengthened the marital bond." Morton Hunt comments on Dr. Stone's statement in his book, *The Affair*, "Perhaps he, like many others with a similar view, came to this conclusion because he saw only troubled clients; perhaps infidelity was more deeply disturbing to many people a generation or so ago than it is today." A more recent study on the results of adultery in our society was conducted by gynecologist Dr. Lonny Meyers and the Reverend Hunter Leggitt. The conclusions they arrived at were published in the journal, *Sexual Behavior*. Based on their interviews they found that an affair enhances some marriages by:

—Lessening the feelings of resentment frequently found within the constraints of long term marriages.

—Removing the burdens of sex and companionship from a spouse who may be exhausted, ill, preoccupied with other matters; or simply not in the mood.

—Increasing the warmth and excitement of one spouse, thereby stimulating the other.

—Motivating a person to become more attractive—to the spouse as well.

—Providing a diversion or temporary respite from marriage difficulties. This can bring a new perspective or tolerance to these problems.

—Assisting a person to discover new dimensions of his or her own sexuality and personality including (for women) orgasm, which may then for the first time be experienced also with the husband.

—Helping an unsatisfactory marriage to remain intact when there are other good reasons to continue the marriage, such as children, finances, and an established home base.

—Allowing persons to remain (or become) warm individuals despite cold marriages.

—By providing additional passion, tenderness, and stimulation for a person experiencing a good marriage.

Dr. Alfred Kinsey, in his volume on the American female, also looked at the other side of the story. He reported and cited three independent studies other than his own to support the statement that "sometimes there is an actual improvement of the marital relationship following extramarital experience." Morton Hunt formed a similar conclusion from his research: "Many psychotherapists and marriage counselors to whom I spoke said, in guarded terms, that stagnant marriages are sometimes stirred into life by the sharp new awareness the unfaithful person had gained of his or her needs, which leads him to make subtle new demands of his spouse and to respond positively when the other meets them." I have confirmed his finding in conversations with my colleagues.

Of the people Hunt interviewed for his book (primarily white middle class, and geographically diverse), a small minority reported improved marital relationships as a result of their affairs:

> About one out of every ten interviewees said their first or some later affair had increased their sexual satisfactions within marriage; roughly the same number said it had brought them emotionally closer to their spouse; and one out of eight said it had strengthened the marriage by turning the partners back toward each other. The improvement seems more likely to be minor, or peripheral, in those cases where the deceived spouse never finds out, more likely to be major and central when the affair has been made known and produced a searching re-evaluation of the whole marital interaction.

Reversals and Renewals

As we saw earlier, when an affair comes out in the open, it is almost always disruptive and usually destructive. But again, there are exceptions. Sometimes the marital partners decide to repair and reconstruct their relationship and come up with a stronger, more mutually nurturant bond than they had before. It is quite possible they might never have done this without the stimulus of the affair.

Allan and Carole have been married thirteen years; four years ago a friend of Carole's told her that Allen was fooling around. At first, she didn't believe it, but when she confronted Allen, he admitted he had had an affair. In taking stock of the past four years, both Carole and Allen are mostly positive:

Carole: When I first found out about Allen's affair, I was shocked. I felt betrayed; it was as if I had been played for a fool. Things were pretty shaky between us for a long while—probably about a year or so. One of the things I had to admit, though, was that I wasn't really cheated. During the time of his affair, Allen wasn't distant and preoccupied, as unfaithful men are depicted in the movies. On the contrary, our sex life was heightened, and he was very affectionate.

Allen: I think that if a person with real integrity, a thoughtful person, feels that the growth of his personality and his happiness and welfare will be promoted by an affair, he should have it, because if he doesn't, he's going to cheat his mate! In the long run, he or she will sense an undercurrent of resentment, a feeling of duty rather than love, that will be more destructive to life than a sexual experience with another, which leaves the lustier one more content within the relationship. Were I deprived of the affair during that period of my life, Carole would have become my enemy. . . . Nonetheless, being found out wasn't a picnic. I think one of the important factors that saved us is that our marriage really didn't have serious shortcomings. Friends of ours whose marriages are already rocky and unsatisfying had experienced extreme turmoil when an affair became an issue, and their marriages never recovered. My guess is that there wasn't much to salvage.

Carole: . . . That first year was like recovering from an accident. Afterward, I came to see Allen and myself in a different light. First of all, I've learned the "wisdom of insecurity." Both men and women have a tendency after marriage to think, "Okay, the romance is over. I can sit back now; I've won him (or her) over." This leads to stagnation. There is a healthy drive toward self-improvement and maybe even a little competitiveness that ceases after marriage. This was revitalized by our marital difficulties.

Allen: In the last few years, I've come to appreciate Carole much more than previously. She has become more independent. I get a strong sense that she doesn't *need* me but she really *wants* me.

She enjoys my company but isn't dependent on it or lost without me. If I
were to disappear, she would be okay
and continue handling her life well. I
didn't sense that four years ago. That
difference is really important to me. . . .
Interestingly enough, nowadays Carole
has orgasms nearly all the time, although before the affair she rarely did.

Carole: I would agree with Allen that I feel
more independent as a person than I
did four years ago, but I don't attribute
it all to our marital difficulties—or at
least not to the affair. What Allen is
overlooking is that four years ago, I had
two preschoolers to deal with. That will
cut down on anyone's independence.
Now that they are both off to school for
a full day, I have started graduate
school, and I can mingle in the civilized
world. Like most mothers, I was going
through a period of isolation and brain
rot while Allen had his usual freedom.
This is one of the things we've rene-
gotiated. The responsibilities for the
children and the house are shared now
. . . . You know, though an extramarital
affair isn't necessarily a disaster, it certainly isn't a panacea either.

Allen: I think you're right, Carole. The point is
that a lot of things that have been very
positive have occurred between us since
that extramarital episode, and even
though other factors may be equally important, the affair also played a critical
role. Not that having an affair is going

> to take anyone to glory, it's just that it doesn't necessarily kill, and in our case may have even provided a motivation for moving closer.

Carole: I agree. I wouldn't claim that we're completely happy now, but I would say that things are definitely better than before it all started.

After an affair is discovered, if the marriage does improve, it will probably do so only after considerable effort and agonizing. While the discovered affair is likely to be traumatic even if marital differences are eventually resolved, marital improvement when the affair is not discovered may come about with less or no trauma. In these cases, the outside experience, serving as a reality test of one's fantasy, may result in a new or renewed appreciation of one's mate. In their book, *The Wandering Husband*, Dr. Hyman Spotnitz and writer Lucy Freeman take the general view that almost all infidelity is psychologically unhealthy. But even these conservatives recognize the exceptions and add, "We can make no ironclad rules, for there are instances where it may have saved a marriage. It may have convinced a husband that the other woman, far from being more desirable, is much less attractive than his wife."

If this insight can apply to wandering husbands, it can also apply to wandering wives. One such woman is Jennifer Lang. Mrs. Lang, at thirty-seven, has been married for eleven years. At first glance, she hardly seems like the sort who would turn to extramarital sex. A second-generation Irish Catholic, she is short and stocky, wears her sweaters a little too loosely, her curly black hair a little too short, and her shoes, chosen for comfort over style, do nothing to improve the appearance of her short muscular legs. Jennifer Lang's experience was expressed in a lengthy letter, which reads in part:

"There was a kind of growing dissatisfaction in my marriage that I couldn't put my finger on. Things were going along smoothly, the kids were doing fine, my husband was making decent money for the first time, and everybody was well. I couldn't understand my moodiness. Now, two years later, I have a better perspective. What happened was that my interests in life had broadened while my husband's had not, and at the same time, I was also moving away from my strong religious background while he remained devout and inhibited. Here I was, placing big value on affection and emotionality, while he seemed opposed to both. I was frustrated. As my discontent grew, I began to wonder what it would be like with another man. I fell into the habit of having long daydreaming sessions. I would even look forward to these private moments with my thoughts. What I did was create a fantasy involving a man with all the qualities I hungered for—openly and passionately emotional, adventurous, uninhibited. We would meet each other, embrace with real passion, and do all sorts of things together. I visualized dinner, dancing closely in each other's arms, kissing and lying tenderly in a soft, romantic embrace. I hardly ever fantasized lovemaking. Although I recognized it as part of the experience, the source of my dissatisfaction was not sexual, it was primarily emotional.

". . . Over the course of three years, I met and got to know five or six men. These are all men that I dated—two of them I slept with. They ranged from a bearded hippie playwright-cab driver to my gynecologist, who asked me out for a drink and with whom I related for a year—longer than any of the others. What I found out after getting to know these men is that my husband is a real find. Although some of these other guys are much more emotional and at times much more fun, this has its negative side. The playwright, for example, was the most affectionate, emotionally stimulating of them all. But on several occasions he didn't show up for dates or was so high that he wasn't coherent by the time he arrived—usually late! Sure, he had a spirited glint in his eye that was appealing, but it wasn't as exciting close up—then it was more bloodshot than sparkle! The gynecologist also had his drawbacks. At first, it was immensely flattering that my doctor found me attractive. I got a lot of ego inflation out of that. But after a while, I found him shallow and superficial. He's a great

companion for dinner and light conversation. He's really an absorbing conversationalist as long as it's kept impersonal. Within
a few months, though, his manner drove me wild. I found myself
trying to reach this guy and he'd put on his frozen Calvinist face
and become polite and monosyllabic. Then there was another
one who sexually was dynamite. But that's all he was interested
in. . . .

"All in all, I've concluded that my ideal of what a man
'should' be needs adjusting. My husband is sincere, responsible,
in love with me, a good father, a sensitive lover, generous—and a
little boring, too security-oriented, and overconventional. Like
everyone else, he has defects. So what! Christ, I've found that he
has more going for him than most men. Those that were more
exciting made horrible steady companions. I can really appreciate that now. The contrast has renewed my respect for my
husband. I don't feel dissatisfied as I did before. Back several
years ago, I felt my choice was to seek other men extramaritally
or to divorce. The option I chose worked for me."

Pronounced Dead

Jennifer Lang's marriage was lacking but viable. In marriages
that are no longer salvageable, the third party may make the
bankruptcy obvious. Before the appearance of the emotion-
al/sexual competition, there were two very unhappy people.
Afterward, with the marital bond formally split, each has a
chance to embark on a new, more satisfying life.

"I'd been thinking about leaving my husband for four years
but I was unsure of myself—afraid to face the single life, afraid of
financial problems, afraid to face my parents, frightened that the
whole thing was a mistake that I would regret forever. My fantasy
was that no one else would ever want me if I left Robert. My
marriage didn't seem worth a damn, but I really didn't have
much basis for comparison. I was married very young—too
young, actually—so I was naive. Also, Robert doesn't like to

have people over and isn't very sociable at all, which cuts down my exposure to other couples. Being naive, underexposed, insecure, and unhappily married was one hell of a sorry state . . . . Our marriage never seemed any good. It included just about zero sex, and as far as I can see, it went on and on not only because of my fears but because of Robert's fears also. He was an up-and-coming corporate lawyer who felt pretense was important; rather than admitting to his colleagues, our parents, and our friends that we couldn't stand each other, he plodded along smiling in public and ignoring me in private—'It's what's up front that counts.'

"One weekend with Phil changed everything. Not that I had any hopes of marrying him—he was too happily married for that. We met at the library several times and one weekend he asked jokingly if I wanted to keep him company on a business trip. He may have been joking, but I wasn't. I jumped at the opportunity. In that one weekend, I learned so much about my own feelings, and my ability to relate to a man on every level. The exhilaration, expansiveness, and sense of discovery that I experienced with Phil gave a new direction to my life. I thought of myself in a completely new way. I almost hugged myself—and cried for all the years I had wasted thinking that I didn't have the capacity to be happy . . . . Sexually, I had never responded as I did with Phil. In my marriage, the lovemaking was wordless, perfunctory, and swift. Phil was a warm and enthusiastic lover. From the moment we touched and kissed, we were pulled to each other; we were key and lock, melody and harmony, cerebral and physical, playful and serious. We made love all weekend. I was never as sharply aware of my sexuality—I was like a wild beast in heat; my body was constantly eager and vibrant. He was only too willing to comply. He rejoiced at the opportunity; it was extraordinarily exciting.

"We made love every night for the following week. On the last night of the week, I broke into tears after I came. I was ready. I went and told my husband everything in a great emotional scene and moved out that same night. I'm living alone now. My marriage is behind me. Sometimes I'm very lonely but I'm happier. The singles scene can be dehumanizing. The bars, clubs, etc.—everything is so plastic. But I have no regrets. I have an exciting job. I've met men I could love, and I feel capable of making myself happy—that was my precious find."

Just as some marriages are exposed in all their sterility by an affair, others, just as empty, may be given artificial life by outside involvements. Rather than face the bleakness of their marriage and courageously arrange for a separation or a divorce, some couples stick their heads in the sand and carry on desultory affairs. After a few years of this, there are often bitter regrets—"I should have ended it when I was younger" or "I've thrown away the best years of my life." Once more, we can see the dual edge of extramarital involvement—it can work both ways, for us or against us.

Playing the Odds: Issue and Answers

We have seen that an affair may be destructive in intent, designed to get rid of a mate; a chance by-product of other marital problems; have little to do with the mate at all; be employed to arouse the partner's interest; be based on revenge for real or fancied hurts; be a way-station on a route back to a more solid marriage. The affair can be a cry for help, a reaching out for health, or the acting out of an inner disturbance. It may be used to prop up a marriage that might better be dissolved, or be the final straw that breaks the bond of a corrupt marriage.

People who have liberal attitudes about adultery in general may surprise themselves when the abstraction becomes a reality in their own marriage. Others, though conservative in theory, may be forgiving and compassionate. Those who respond initially with mild upset may have a more serious delayed reaction. Some partners are truly devastated and rocked to the very foundations of their personality.

We know now that there are many kinds of marriage and

many kinds of adultery, that all monogamy is not blissful and healthy and that all adultery is not painful and sick. The partner who is having an affair may become more open, more in touch with his feelings. At the time of the affair, he may make a greater effort to please the other partner, thereby affecting a temporary (and occasionally a lasting) improvement in the relationship. Variety may be introduced into the marital sex life by the unfaithful partner who has gained a new sexual outlook or learned some new techniques. Some unfaithful partners develop a stronger appreciation and love for their spouses as a result of extramarital activity. These are the potential positive effects of an affair. Suspicion, anger, distrust, guilt, and even divorce are common negative effects. In a traditional marriage without close communication between the mates, more negative disruption tends to occur if the wife's affair is discovered. If the husband has an affair, less harm seems to result.

What sense can we make of these seeming contradictions? An affair tends to make life more exciting; whether or not it satisfies, produces conflict, destroys, or uncovers a new dimension of personality it certainly intensifies life. Beyond that, we can only say one thing with certainty: all general conclusions are likely to have notable exceptions!

Some marriages gain from adultery, others lose; some mates grow, others deteriorate; sometimes the effects of an affair are temporary and of no real consequence, other times they have critical impact and are long-lasting. There are very few reliable scientific studies on this issue. With a few exceptions, those that have been done have sampled populations that are either biased in a liberal or conservative direction, depending on the consequences the questioner wanted to emphasize. This is not legitimate research. More objective evidence and clinical investigation of nonpatient populations by and large echo the conclusions we have drawn in earlier chapters: That adultery *must* adversely affect a marriage or that it is always a symptom of a troubled marriage or troubled psyche is a myth. It is not having an affair in itself that counts but the state of the marriage, the motivation of the adulterer, the self-image of the noninvolved spouse (particularly if the affair is discovered), and the meaning the affair holds for both spouses.

Considering all these factors, the majority of professionals who have published opinions and I myself conclude that prolonged extramarital experiences result in decidely more negative than positive effects on a marriage. Again, this need not be so, but for most people it is. Perhaps you can beat the odds. Perhaps not. In a mutually tender, loving marriage, the stakes rise—there is more to lose and less to gain. Yet paradoxically, the likelihood of losing a truly solid relationship is smaller. In a nonsatisfactory relationship that one desires to keep intact, there is less to lose and more to gain—but if found out, the likelihood is that the marital facade will quickly drop. These are the extremes; most marriages lie in between.

Improving the
Marital Relationship

What Once Was

The scene is an exclusive seaside restaurant. A couple in their mid-forties are having dinner. He is deeply tanned, prosperous looking. She, a former model, now a Ph.D. candidate in English literature, has bright green eyes and a lightly freckled face under a fluff of reddish-brown hair. They have been married eighteen years. They are aware of each other but only vaguely. This night, as on many others, their attention is directed elsewhere; presently their eyes and ears are trained on a younger couple seated nearby—a man and a women locked in each other's gaze, speaking softly, inaudibly, sometimes laughing together, other times looking very serious, playful, and earnest, all the while holding hands.

The older couple, disconnected for many years, share a silent thought: Were we ever like that? If we were, what happened? How did the bottom fall out? The bottom, of course, did not suddenly fall out. Relationships do not suddenly collapse. Life is a process. People don't break, they slowly melt. This man and woman, who once thought they had it made, failed or refused to recognize the signals flashed over nearly two decades that they hadn't. They continue together in desperation, ignoring their failure to communicate and to share. There is a marked absence of empathy—the single most important ingredient of intimacy. Failing over and over again to feel for each other, their feelings have turned into the resentful hatred of the trapped or the muted boredom of the habitual.

Marriages crumble, finally, when each blames the other for failing to live up to the original visions that impelled the alignment: "I would have made something of myself had it not been for you!" or "I could have married someone who would have made me happy. Why did I choose you?" The "why" is probably unanswerable. Analysis brings, at best, conjectured responses: A man may want a hostess, a mother, an accessory, a centerfold, a sister, a slave, or a tyrant. A woman may crave a father, a son, a savior, an escape from home. Few of us marry out of mature love. We marry out of hope, and we hope that our fantasies will spring to life. We dream of love, but developing a loving relationship is another matter. Marriage, involving two complex and ever-changing adults and, in most instances, one or more equally complex and rapidly changing children, precludes continuous and perfect harmony. This is impossible. It is possible, however, to achieve a reasonably nurturing, loving, and workable relationship despite the inherent flaws of the institution. Most marriages, unfortunately, do not achieve this; they are more often characterized by discord and destructiveness.

Reversing the trend in a marriage and taking steps toward learning to work as a team is not easy. When an affair either comes out in the open or, undiscovered, is symptomatic of a poorly functioning relationship, the marital partners may decide to repair and reconstruct their relationship. Some couples try it on their own, others with professional help. Even with the support of a well-trained mental health practitioner, considerable time and effort are usually required to achieve change. Patience, courage, and most of all, the desire to change are key ingredients. Given these factors, the "do it yourself" material that follows still will not guarantee fidelity, a perfect marriage, or even a workable one. However, if the suggestions are studied and seriously applied, several things are likely to occur:

1. Old destructive patterns of relating will not be so frequently activated.
2. Small problems will not become big problems as often.
3. Certain "touchy" areas of the relationship will be explored more satisfactorily than previously.
4. Relationship-defeating motivations for extramarital sex such as hostility, emotional alienation, and misunderstanding will become less probable.

A reminder: If, because of extramarital activity (or other painful deceptions), serious suspicion and mistrust abound in a relationship, a tension may develop that will not necessarily be dispelled by the remedies that follow. As an example of this tension, the unknowing (but sometimes vaguely suspicious) partner may be taken by surprise and react defensively to the "let's work on our marriage" attitude of the unfaithful spouse. Or, feeling deprived and cheated, the faithful spouse may seize the opportunity to be openly angry and demeaning. When the saving effort is consistently ill received, trust has been seriously eroded and professional help may be warranted.

Confusing Each Other

Communication in marriage is a constant. When husband and wife can hear or observe each other, there is the potential for an exchange of information. By verbal means or through bodily or facial expressions, messages are sent. The information contained in a message may be straightforward and factual, conveyed by words—"I want to eat" or "I put gas in the car" or "It is cold"—or the tone of voice or gesture may indicate something more complex. Sometimes the meaning of a message is hard to decipher. This is particularly true when indirectness and subtlety play a major role in the marital relationship. When messages are hidden and indirect, husbands and wives typically develop habits of assuming that they understand what their mates mean by certain actions or feel in certain situations, or intend by various words or gestures or tone of voice. Frequently they are wrong. Acting on the erroneous assumption, however, will often trigger a mate to respond negatively, thus reaffirming and further entrenching the "mind reader's" position that he was "right in the first place."

Janet and Dan have been married three years. They were both married before. When Dan was still married to his first wife, he had an affair with Janet, who was divorced. Although Dan and Janet were both touched by their brief encounter (it happened during one of Dan's business trips) it was not pursued at the time because of Dan's marriage. Two months later, Dan's wife left him for another man. Six months after that, Dan and Janet were married. Because he slept with her while he was still married to his first wife, Janet worries that Dan will have affairs while married to her. She is secretly suspicious of him. Dan regards his action in his previous marriage as an exception to his usual behavior. He views the motivation of his affair with Janet as desperation. His marriage had been deteriorating for a long time and he acted quite out of his usual character. He operates from a standpoint of fidelity and trust with Janet. She, in turn, is guided by mistrust and her suspicious attitude—"If he did it to his previous wife, he will probably do it to me." Consequently, their discussions about leaves from home, particularly business trips, are filled with misunderstanding:

> Janet: You know what, I think I'll go to Chicago with you, Dan. Maybe I can be of some help to you there.
>
> Dan: That's okay Jan, I'm provided with a nice hotel room, meals, transportation, and so on. I don't really need any help.
>
> Janet: (disappointed) Oh, then I can keep you company.

Dan: (starting to experience a vague sense of guilt) Jan, it's nice of you to want to be with me, but my schedule keeps me busy from 9 A.M. to midnight, and it wouldn't be appropriate for you to sit in on business meetings, so I would hardly see you.

Janet: (persistent with a trace of annoyance in her voice) I think I'd like to go anyway.

Dan: (impatient and annoyed) Listen, the company won't pay your way, and I would hardly see you, so there's no point in spending an extra five hundred dollars that we can ill afford for nothing. Let's leave it at that.

Janet: Let's not leave it at that. I'm going!

Dan: (angry and frustrated) Shit! Janet, for Christ's sake, when you get so damned unreasonable, I feel as if I don't know you anymore. You're not like the woman I married.

Janet: (her anxiety and resentment escalating) That's it! You don't want to be with me anymore. I knew it! You're looking for someone else . . . .

Conversations based on indirectness and private, untested assumptions such as Janet's and Dan's are frequently disastrous. In this instance, Dan assumed Janet was merely being pig-headed. Janet, of course, assumed Dan, cornered, was being purposely evasive. Had she directly stated her concern or had Dan asked why the trip was so important, the outcome might have been different. It is probable that these patterns of behavior are present to a degree in almost all marriages: There is an argument, the source of which is unclear or camouflaged; the result after many futile bouts is often of the you-hurt-me-so-I'll-hurt-you variety; in many instances, vindictiveness becomes the major force in the gradual weakening of the relationship.

As the negativeness created by indirectness escalates, it mushrooms into other areas of the relationship. That is, once a negative, destructive atmosphere of misunderstanding is established, more indirectness and misunderstanding are likely to follow as protection against the "enemy." For example, an individual such as Janet may begin to attack Dan on any number of insignificant issues—his dress, his manners, his parenting, and so on. In actuality, Janet's disturbance is related to something entirely different—she is insecure and afraid of losing Dan. Stating her real concern in the attack-counter-attack atmosphere of her own making, however, would be too painful. Instead she is caught in a series of relationship-defeating attempts to allay her anxiety and keep Dan off balance.

There is no guaranteed way to avoid misunderstanding with a spouse but one thing is sure—coaxing, cajoling, dropping "cute" hints, manipulating, and beating around the bush are all barriers to clear communication. "Did you pick up the groceries today?" Alice asks John. Since John has arrived home without the groceries, Alice's question didn't have to be asked. What she was saying was "Why are you so late? I wish you had picked up the groceries." Or John may say to Alice, after spending the evening at the home of friends, "Mary certainly comes up with unusual meals, doesn't she?" What John is really conveying by his tone of voice, though, is more like, "Why don't you cook a few more interesting dishes?"

When something is wanted, be it change, clarification, reassurance, companionship, or support, it is important that the message be direct and to the point. Speaking in generalities won't get the job done.

A couple has just come out of the water after a delightful moonlight swim. The woman says, "Let's go inside. I'm sleepy." The man responds, "It's nice out here. Why don't we lie and rest here." The woman, angry, storms into the house. The man, equally angry, drives off to a local bar. What happened? She, by saying she was "sleepy," was actually signaling her desire to make love in the house. He, ironically, was signaling his desire to make love in the moonlight. Neither said what he or she wanted directly. Both felt rejected by each other. The evening ended in anger and hurt, rather than pleasure. Preventing this unfortunate turn of events may have been as simple as saying, "Let's go inside, I'm in the mood to make love," or "It's nice out here, why don't we make love in the moonlight?"

Feeling Talk

Once a couple begins to communicate so that the intended message is received unambiguously, the next task—attention to feelings—can be approached. It is easy to misread or overlook feelings. This indifference starts in childhood when many of us learn to keep our mouths shut and hide our feelings. Later, when we go to school, we learn about math, geography, and grammar, but feelings are rarely part of the curriculum. As adults, we are busy; we have goals to reach, achievements to attain, and days pass quickly without much attention to feelings. Your job may be shaky, one of your children may be sick, and you may have a cold coming on—but if a casual friend asks in passing how you feel, you will probably reply, "I'm fine." This kind of superficial exchange is merely a sign of friendliness, not an expression of feelings. Life is full of such rituals—harmless small talk. The trouble is that over the years these shallow, habitual responses become so ingrained that we devalue the importance of our own feelings and those of the significant people in our lives.

A lifetime of inattentiveness to feelings is strikingly demonstrated by Martin, a musician, and Gloria, his wife of twenty years. Two months before this conversation, Gloria had discovered Martin's long-standing infidelity:

> Martin: I don't think we've ever been a team in-
> timately. I've never felt close to you. I've

always felt you were my doll. You were my gracious hostess, my lovely lady, my bride. But I don't think I ever made total love to you. I loved you with reservation. As though you were a piece of art and would surely break if I were to release my passion on you and in you. So, throughout the years, I've sought to release this passion with other women.

Therapist: Gloria, how did you feel about the relationship all these years?

Gloria: How did I feel? Well . . . I suppose lonely. I wanted to be with Martin more. I wanted to be more passionate with him; less reserved, but I always felt he would reject me. I always felt he wanted me up on a pedestal. I stayed there to keep him.

Martin: (stunned) But, Gloria, I never knew that. Why didn't you tell me how you felt? Why didn't you say something?

Gloria: Afraid, I guess. You never asked. I thought that was the way you wanted things.

Therapist: Martin, how come you never said anything?

Martin: (crying) For the same reasons, I suppose. I took it for granted that Gloria was happy with the status quo. I didn't want to hurt her or be hurt. God, I wish I had known how you felt back then, Gloria. I didn't really want to see other women. I wanted intimacy. Closeness. We could have given that to each other.

The waste of time, energy, and potential happiness through the years of Martin and Gloria's marriage, when what they both *really* wanted was so much more similar than what they each *supposed* the other wanted, is appalling. Yet this same kind of waste affects millions of marriages. A main cause is the failure of husbands and wives to be attuned to each other's feelings. To understand another person's thoughts and feelings thoroughly, and to be thoroughly understood by this other person in return —this is one of the most rewarding of human experiences, and unfortunately, all too rare. In another example, we will see how a couple interact ineffectively and how the same issues can be discussed more sensitively.

Judy and Jerry have been married for eight years. They have two children, five and six. Jerry is an executive in a large electronics firm. He has a good job and they live very comfortably. Jerry drives home from work on a summer evening and is greeted at the door by an exuberant Judy.

> Judy: Hi, sweetheart. I've got great news.
>
> Jerry: Terrific. What's up?
>
> Judy: I could hardly wait until tonight to tell you. Remember how I've mentioned my boredom and feeling of uselessness in the past? Well, today I did something about it. I went over to the college, filled out an application form, and had an interview for the nursing program. I was told my chances for acceptance are very good and it is likely I'll be starting in September. I'm so excited.
>
> Jerry: (angrily) What about the kids? What about your responsibilities here? How the hell can you start school with all that? Nothing doing! We don't need extra expenses and more chaos!

Judy: (angry and defensive) Who the hell do you think you are? You can't live my life for me. I'm bored; I want something meaningful to do and I'm going back to school.

Jerry: Oh no you aren't.

Judy: Oh yes I am!

Jerry: I won't let you. I'm not going to give you the money.

Judy: That won't stop me. You bastard! I'll borrow the money. I'm tired of being bored, depressed, and burdened. No one's going to stop me from taking care of myself.

Jerry: Is that all you think you are, a house-wife?

Judy: No. I'm much more. I'm a babysitter, cook, window-washer, waxer, cleaner, and clerk—and I've had it. I start school next month and that's all there is to it!

Jerry: You can't.

Judy: I can and I am. That's final.

Jerry: You're not and that's final!

Here's a replay of this couple's conversation, this time with each recognizing and respecting the other's feelings:

Judy: Hi, sweetheart. I've got great news.

Jerry: You really seem excited. What's up?

Judy: I am excited. I could hardly wait until tonight to tell you. Today I finally did something to counter the boredom and sense of uselessness I've been experiencing. I went over to the college, filled out the application forms, and had an interview for the nursing program. I was told my chances for acceptance are very good and it is likely I'll be starting in September.

Jerry: Gee, you really seem high about this. I wish I could share your enthusiasm about going back to school, but I have mixed feelings about it.

Judy: Mixed feelings? I don't understand. Why are your feelings mixed?

Jerry: I'm not sure; it's so sudden, I haven't had a chance to think about it . . . . On the one hand, I'm glad you're enthused about something. I know you've been down in the dumps for a while. But there's something frightening to me about this. I also feel funny that something as important to you as going back to school wasn't discussed with me until now.

Judy: It sounds as if you were really thrown by this. It really is kind of sudden. I've been thinking about it for a few days, and when I decided to do it, I wanted to surprise you. It seems I shocked you instead.

Jerry: You did. That's for sure. There are lots of things that scare me about this.

Judy: For example?

Jerry: What about the kids? Are they going to be short-changed?

Judy: Well, both of them are going to be in school in the fall. I met with a counselor today and planned a tentative course schedule that doesn't conflict with their school hours. I'll be able to make it home substantially before them in the afternoon.

Jerry: Boy, you've really planned this thing out. It must mean a great deal to you.

Judy: It does. It is vitally important to me. And so are you and the children. But I recognize that I have been restless and out of sorts for a long time now. I have been inattentive to myself and my own needs. I've been bored. There is no challenge in my life.

Jerry: You aren't satisfied with the loving feelings we all have for you?

Judy: I am, Jerry. But it isn't enough. We all have strong feelings for you. Would you be satisfied to stop work, stay home, and be a "housefather?"

Jerry: Come on now. You know that wouldn't be enough for me.

Judy: I feel the same way. It's not that these other things aren't important, but I miss the stimulation of the world outside of this house.

Jerry: I have to say this Judy, I'm also worried that you'll be less available to me when you start school.

Judy: It's true that I'll probably be busier and have less time for you, Jerry. But I'll have a renewed zest for life. I think this will be communicated to you and the children. I believe I can be a better person and, consequently, a better mother by not ignoring my development.

Jerry: You present a pretty convincing case, Judy, but I can't say that I'm totally comfortable with the idea. I appreciate how important this venture is to you and I respect your right to pursue it. I realize that if I were in your place, I would do the same thing.

Judy: I understand this is a transition for you as well as for me, Jerry, and there may be some difficulties that will have to be worked out. But I'm confident things will fall into place.

In this couple's first conversation, they quickly became adversaries. Their dialogue was primarily authoritarian and judgmental ("We don't need extra expenses and more chaos!"); threatening and counterthreatening ("I'm not going to give you the money." "No one's going to stop me . . ."). This kind of dialogue hardly ever produces a resolution of the issue at hand, and both parties are likely to storm off bitter and resentful. The all too familiar result of this kind of exchange—which may be yelled, signaled by angry glances, or telegraphed by hurt silence —is: "Everything would have worked out fine if you hadn't upset me" or "You just don't give a damn about my feelings." Building trust and resolving important personal issues satisfactorily requires recognition of and respect for a spouse's feelings and point of view. These qualities were conspicuously lacking in the first dialogue.

In the replay dialogue, although Judy and Jerry were not in

total agreement about the issue (" . . . I can't say I am comfortable about the idea"), they communicated an understanding of each other's position and feelings ("It must mean a great deal to you" and "This is a transition for you as well as for me, Jerry"). It was as if they were silently asking, "How does he (she) see it; how does he (she) feel; how would I feel if this were said to me?" This is empathy, a critical ingredient in marriages that mutually satisfy. It is an effort to understand another's beliefs, practices, and feelings without necessarily sharing or agreeing with them. While empathy does not require agreement with the other's view, it does preclude the demand that "You must think, feel, and act like me." This may seem an unnecessary statement, but empathy is actually a radical departure from usual relating. Many of us are unaware of the tremendous pressure we put on our wives, husbands, children, to have the same feelings we do. It is often as though we silently say, "If you want me to love you, then you must have the same feelings I do. If I feel your behavior is bad, you must feel so too. If I feel a certain goal is desirable, you must feel so too."

Empathy is made up of two main factors. One is listening and attempting to understand another's view rather than busily preparing a rebuttal. The second is communicating this understanding to the speaker. A small exercise that frequently helps to develop this pattern of communicating is "role reversal." In this exercise, when a discussion involving differences or personal/emotional issues occurs, it becomes the responsibility of each spouse to state the partner's position and feelings until he is satisfied with the degree of understanding. If he is not satisfied with the level of understanding, a brief "time-out" is called while his position and related feelings are expressed again. The discussion does not proceed until each partner is satisfied that the salient aspects of his position are understood. For example:

Husband: I'm out there all day long, getting one turndown after another. Being a salesman is tough. Some days it really gets to me.

Wife: Cooking and cleaning—that's my day. What the hell are you complaining about?

Husband: Hold it. Time out! You passed right over my feelings. Can you please restate what I said from *my* viewpoint. (Husband is asking for an empathic response.)

Wife: It sounded as if you were trying to make me feel guilty, and I won't have any of that. (Rather than looking at his feelings, wife is still focusing on her own.)

Husband: That wasn't my intention. I was just feeling a bit frustrated. Do you understand? (Husband is restating his position and asking her to express *his* position in her own words.)

Wife: I understand now. You are feeling frustrated after a day of rejections. It's just that I had a lousy day also.

Husband: Sounds like you're also pretty frustrated. What's the matter? . . .

If a husband and wife will conscientiously make certain to perform this exercise even though it may seem forced and silly at the beginning, many difficulties not caused by actual differences but by misunderstanding and emotional alienation will be prevented. What's more, when feelings are identified and expressed in an empathic manner, a couple will sometimes find that the real difficulty has little to do with what they are arguing about. An argument about flirting at social gatherings, for instance, might be only a symptom of two people's assumptions: "If you loved me, you wouldn't do this" or "If you respected me, you'd trust me." The fears behind the assumption are quite similar: "I'm afraid you don't love/respect me." At this level, seeming differences turn into shared experience. That is, each partner might feel emotionally threatened by the flirting or the command to stop, and the surface disagreement may only be an expression of the differences in the way each partner avoids or copes with very similar feelings and experiences. Only by being sensitive to each other's feelings will a couple achieve a level of disscussion where these discoveries occur.

Since it is just when emotions are strongest that it is most difficult to achieve empathic communication, a third party, such as a close friend, who is able to lay aside his own feelings and evaluations, can assist greatly by listening with understanding to each person and clarifying the views and attitudes each holds. When the individuals in the dispute realize they are being understood, that someone sees how the situation seems to them, the statements are likely to grow less exaggerated and defensive, and it is no longer necessary to maintain the attitude, "I am one hundred percent right and you are one hundred percent wrong." Along with decreased defensiveness comes a clarification of the issues, which opens the path toward resolution. Obviously, though, if the issue is never explored in depth, if superficiality is maintained by mutual recrimination and insult, the likelihood of successful resolution is minimal.

Obstacles

A married couple has a fight. It begins because the wife feels irritated with her husband about something. They go to bed that evening without saying a word to each other. She is no longer angry and would like her husband to contact her, talk to her, reach out to her, caress her. He, not knowing that her mood has passed and fearing that she is still upset, does nothing of the sort, deciding to wait it out until she gives some indication of reacting to him more kindly. She is not willing to reach out and make contact herself, although she would like to. Lying there, she begins to blame him for not "making a move"—for not doing something she herself is unwilling to do.

A wife feels ill at ease going to a restaurant, theater, or any public place unaccompanied. She asks her husband to take her to a movie. He would rather watch a football game on television, and suggests she go alone and that afterward they meet for dinner. She responds with, "Why are you so selfish?" and refuses to speak to him all evening.

Tom was a very poor manager of money. His debts piled up unpaid. His one major avenue to recovery was to file for a substantial federal income tax refund dating back several years. Tom procrastinated despite his wife's pleading. The bills piled up, adding more pressure to their daily grind. Finally, Tom filed for his refund and received a prompt reply from the Internal Revenue Service stating that his request exceeded the cut off date and was no longer valid. Tom immediately blamed his wife, Betty, saying she should "have kept after him." When Betty grew angry and told him that his failure to get things done was driving her to distraction, Tom continued to deny personal responsibility and escalated the blame to a new level. "If it was that important to you," he said, "why didn't you lock me out of the house or something until I filed the return?"

In all the above examples, the blamer has the attitude, "I'm not responsible, you are." From this follows: "If you are responsible for my (our) discomfort, distress, or unhappiness, only you can alter it." The following statements are characteristic of this attitude:

"If you treated me as though you really loved me, I could accomplish anything."

"If you would only accomplish something, I could really love you."

"If you would only make me welcome, I'd be home all the time and I'd be loving."

"If you stopped going golfing so often and stay home more, I wouldn't act so nasty."

"If only you didn't drink so much, I wouldn't be so bitchy."

"If you weren't so bitchy, I wouldn't drink so much."

"If you encouraged me instead of condemning me, I would be a success."

"If you would only do things right, I would be so appreciative."

"If you were only more informed and well read, I would have more to say to you."

"If only you paid attention to me and showed me my opinion counts, I would feel more confident in expressing it."

"If you didn't interrupt me whenever I starting talking, I'd feel my remarks were more worthwhile and be more sociable with your friends."

"If only you wouldn't embarrass me in front of my friends, I wouldn't be so hostile."

"If only you'd stop pampering the children, I would become more involved in parenting."

"If only you'd become more involved with the children, I wouldn't have to be both mother and father to them."

"If you'd hold my hand and pay attention to me at parties, I'm sure I'd never flirt again in my life."

"If only you weren't such a flirt at parties, I wouldn't have to compete for your attention."

If it would help the marriage for the wife to be less flirtatious and the husband more attentive at parties, who is to take the initiative? And will the person making the first move be regarded by the spouse as having been wrong all along? When couples relate in such a blame-oriented way, they are involved in the major obstacle to relating. Direct and empathic communication will not occur if both husband and wife are constantly screaming or silently sulking about who is to blame. Resolution is unlikely unless one partner is willing to take on-the-spot initiative.

Typically, in the blame-counterblame trap, both partners issue their complaints *after* the unwanted behavior but do nothing while it is taking place. A husband may accuse his wife of being inconsiderate because she repeatedly interrupts him. He will nag, complain, sulk, and admonish—but rarely will he take a firm stand while the behavior is actually happening. What if he stated while being interrupted, "You're interrupting me, Barbara. Please let me finish what I'm saying." If this didn't work, he might simply get up and leave the room, saying, "It seems, by your constant interruptions, that you are not interested in what I'm saying. When you feel more like listening, let me know." Although this behavior may seem harsh, it would probably work.

Jane harbors resentment toward Bill because he doesn't pay attention to her at social gatherings. Yet this behavior has continued on Bill's part for a long period of time, so it is likely she has been blaming and antagonizing him rather than taking responsibility for getting what she wants—more attention. Perhaps she goes off in a corner at parties or gets nasty and sarcastic about Bill's social adroitness. Later, when they are alone, she may sulk or explode and tell Bill his behavior makes her furious, so that their conflict escalates into a fight or mutual withdrawal. If Jane would take responsibility for her shyness, envy of her husband's social popularity, desire for more attention, or whatever, instead of waiting for him to "save her," a major stumbling block to a functional marriage would be removed. This might involve an immediate cessation of blaming statements, working to overcome her social shyness, and making a concerted effort to be part of her husband's conversations instead of withdrawing. Jane's initiative could break the cycle of mutual recrimination and restore the opportunity for productive communication.

You Do for Me, I'll Do for You: Compromise and Exchange

When mutual blaming and accusations are not a major issue and communication is becoming more direct and empathic, a husband and wife are in a good position to bargain, negotiate, and work at compromises in their relationship. To some people, *bargaining* and *negotiating* are terms to be applied to business not marriage. In marriage, writers of popular magazine articles argue, people should "make sacrifices," "give for giving's sake," "do it for him," "be more loving," etc. These admonitions ignore that most marriage partners have different tastes, attitudes, behaviors, and goals, and that these differences can be resolved only on the basis of mutually understood "rules of exchange."

Charles and Joan, a couple in their late twenties, operate within the framework of what might be described as a "traditional" marriage. Joan is considerate of and expresses her affection for Charles, takes primary responsibility for the children, prepares meals and cleans the house. When asked why she does these things, Joan replies, "Because I love Charles."

Joan may indeed love Charles, but she engages in these behaviors in exchange for certain behaviors from Charles. He is considerate of her and expresses his affection for her; he provides their income, makes household repairs, and takes care of the cars. If these behaviors were to stop, would there be a change in Joan's behavior? Quite likely. Very rarely are individuals so complementary in tastes and desires that negotiating and compromising are not required. For the rest of us, scores of conflicts are inevitable unless we have a good understanding of what our mates expect to get and give in return. When this understanding is lacking or the giving and getting cease to be reciprocal, bitterness, resentment, and general unhappiness usually result.

Morris and Evelyn have been married for four years. For the first three years of their marriage, they both worked, Morris as an engineer, Evelyn as a teacher. During those three years, Morris and Evelyn shared a common goal—purchasing a home—which they accomplished. At the end of their third year of marriage, two things happened: Evelyn gave birth and Morris received a substantial promotion. As a result of these events, Morris and Evelyn experienced a dramatic change in their usual routine. Evelyn left her teaching position and was at home all day caring for her child. Morris was home less because of his increased responsibility. When Morris returned home, he was sometimes irritable and usually quite fatigued. Often, he was greeted by a wife who felt equally off color. To prepare himself for the unpleasant news and growing friction at home, Morris began to stop for a drink after work. Evelyn, disgusted with the unpredictability of his arrival home, stopped preparing meals. Morris, in turn, began eating out more frequently. They were becoming more and more distant:

> Morris: It used to be that we sat down, had cocktails and a leisurely meal together. We would discuss our day and enjoy each other's company. Then I came home and the house was a mess, the meal was lousy, and I was greeted by a tiger ready to lunge at me.

> Evelyn: I felt Morris no longer had any interest in me. He seemed to have more interest in his business. When he came home, all he wanted to do was eat quickly, watch TV, and go to sleep. When I suggested that we go out together after the baby went to sleep, he constantly refused because he was tired. Well, I was tired also, but I desperately needed some stimulation.

> Morris: We seemed to have lost our coordination. For example, with sex, Evelyn felt that I was interested only when I was horny and unresponsive to her needs when she felt sexy. As a result, we hardly had sex anymore.

Both Evelyn and Morris felt they weren't getting a just return for their efforts. Morris felt that his difficulties in coping with the pressures of his new position weren't appreciated. Evelyn felt that Morris did not recognize the difficulties of her adjustment. Day after day, night after night, both Evelyn and Morris sought to exert power over each other, to reap his or her "fair share." Fortunately, having a sound relationship and the basis for good communication, they eventually saw the futility of their struggle and agreed to work things out through compromise. Their attitudes sitting down together could be characterized thus: "I can't have everything I want and you can't have everything you want, so let's compromise in such a manner that we each have those things that are most important, and at the same time let us each try to foster the well-being of the other to the maximum extent possible."

Sadly, most couples are either unaware of such a workable "exchange attitude" or merely pay it lip service. As a result, their many differences with regard to food preferences, moods, sex, types of entertainment, choice of friends, responsibility for household tasks, extramarital involvements, personal habits (e.g., smoking and drinking), and employed activity (e.g., working late or on weekends) are a constant source of friction. The message they convey to each other seems to be, "If you won't change for me, then I won't change for you." In contrast, those couples who live by the tenets of mutual exchange—compromise, recognition of individuality, and compassion—are more likely to discuss issues of conflict, not as adversaries, but as partners, and thus avoid endless unnecessary bickering. The message they convey to each other seems to be: "You scratch my back and I'll scratch yours."

Here are some of the agreements Evelyn and Morris worked out: Morris agreed to abstain from an after-work stopover for a drink. Evelyn agreed not to "close in" on Morris as soon as he arrived home but to allow him time to shower and take a short nap. Evelyn arranged for a babysitter and was also able to nap and refresh herself in the early evening. They both agreed to eat a late dinner together after the baby was asleep. One night a week was set aside for going out for dinner and entertainment.

During their discussions, Morris recognized that Evelyn's moods and behavior were greatly influenced by his acknowledging her as a capable homemaker and desirable wife, and that this acknowledgment must go beyond the form of doing something for her; rather, it would most effectively be a personal demonstration that he loves and admires her as a person, and that she is as important to him as his work. Morris's plan included two elements: expressing his appreciation of Evelyn more often; and increasing his involvement in household responsibilities including sitting down with Evelyn and working out tactics for making life easier.

Morris also suggested to Evelyn that if their relationship did not improve as a result of the numerous exchange agreements, he would consider changing to a less demanding job. Evelyn was profoundly touched by Morris's offer. She recognized the significance of his statement and told him so. She added that his interest and appreciation made her work more acceptable and a job change was unnecessary. She also began to express more interest in his work.

Whenever differences occur, whether between spouses, business partners, or nations, they are resolved in only three ways: One party attempts domination (result: hostility, war); mutual or unilateral withdrawal (result: divorce, isolation); mutual compromise (result: something for something). If individuals are seeking a more satisfying relationship with each other rather than divorce or aggression, mutual exchange or compromise clearly offers the greatest promise. Severe and long-lasting differences may require professional assistance for successful resolution.

Here are some suggestions for renegotiating and compromising moderately abrasive differences before they become severe:

1. A mutual agreement that the communication skills discussed earlier are adequate and operative is a prerequisite. Without this ability, bargaining is very likely to break down and worsen rather than improve the relationship. If, after a reasonable period of attempting to improve com-

munication skills, there is no progress, professional help should be considered.

2. Choose a time and make a formal appointment with each other for the compromise-exchange discussion. Pick an hour when interruptions are unlikely. An ideal time is when both partners will be unhurried and relaxed. If there are several postponements of meetings, this may be an indication that one or both partners are avoiding a confrontation. Discuss this issue.

3. Each spouse should state very specifically what he or she would like or desire and avoid vague generalities. For example, "I would like greater closeness" is too broad. More specific statements that would be instructive to a mate might be: "I would like to eat dinner together" or "I would like to spend time each evening discussing the day's events."

4. Begin with what is wanted rather than what is not wanted. Since both partners may have the tendency to use the exchange session as a forum for condemning the other, it is wise to focus on increasing desired behavior until confidence in the procedure and in each other is established. For example, "I would like more statements of appreciation" is positive, whereas "I want you to stop picking on me as you have been" may lead to an argument. Avoid evaluative, right-and-wrong types of statements. Consider differences as just what they are—differences.

5. Avoid using outside standards to express what is wanted. There is less likelihood of resistance when other people's standards are not used as levers. For instance, rather than saying "Why can't you be like Ed Jones," simply state what you want without reference to Jones.

6. When the change requested is outside the behavioral repertoire of a partner, steps to improve or gain the behavior should include a plan for mutual involvement. For example if both decide that the husband needs more schooling to increase his earning power, perhaps the wife will take a part-time job while he expands his education.

7. Do not try to negotiate feelings. Feelings are not usually

changed by bargaining—"Okay, I agree to be happy about your affair" just won't work. Only behaviors can be negotiated; and only those behaviors that do not compromise a person's integrity are open to negotiation.

8. Be patient. Compromise and exchange agreements are difficult. Do not expect to arrive at a mutual agreement immediately. Several discussion sessions may be necessary even on seemingly mild issues.

Keeping the Dialogue Alive: The Marital Checkup

Most people do not actively attempt to prevent marital discord. When the relationship is in deep trouble and about to blow up, then, and only then, will they attempt to examine the difficulty. Even when a crisis is occurring, one or both parties may still attempt to deny the worsening condition. Pretending that a problem does not exist, however, is not often a lasting solution. For one thing, the amount of work—energy, strength, time—required to support a conspiracy of denial regarding a poorly functioning relationship is at least equal to that required to build a working relationship. For another, as a marriage deteriorates, the probability that it can be improved lessens.

One way couples can counter the tendency to allow problems to continue too long is by instituting the marital checkup. Just as our bodies and automobiles are routinely checked and inspected, marriages may also be given checkups. One vehicle for a marital checkup is a questionnaire responded to jointly. The questions that follow are intended to assist a couple in identifying and appraising marital liabilities and assets. A specific scoring system is not used; rather, the responses, given out loud in each other's presence, will serve as stimuli for continuing discussion.

INSTRUCTIONS

Each spouse is to take turns at being the first to answer a question. The answers should be kept brief, with no comment given until each partner has had a chance to respond fully. Comments are to be limited to clarification. This will enable a couple to go through the entire procedure in one sitting and to obtain an impression of qualities and defects of the relationship. Preferably within one week, the couple can arrange to go over the questions again. This time each question is discussed more fully in terms of satisfaction/dissatisfaction, and solutions may be attempted using the principles of communication and compromise-exchange outlined earlier.

Marital Checkup
1. Is rejoining your spouse at the close of the day a pleasant event? If not, discuss the most important reason for regarding your mate's return home as unpleasant. Be specific; for example, "Very often I return home to screaming children and immediate pressure from my wife to step in and settle disputes"; "As soon as my husband walks in he gives me the third degree: 'Did you pick up the clothes, make those calls, walk the dog,' and so on. I feel as if I have to stand inspection every evening."
2. Which aspect of your life gives you the most pleasure or stimulation: your marriage, your work, your children, your hobbies, or some other area? Why?
3. Describe five satisfactory aspects of your marriage.
4. Is your sex life satisfactory to you? If not, what suggestions would you offer for improvement?
5. Name five instances in the past month when you have expressed appreciation of your mate.
6. Name five things your mate has done for you in the past month for which you felt appreciative.
7. Recall three negative things that you have done—-intentionally or unintentionally—to your mate in the last month. How could these occurrences have been prevented?
8. Recall three negative things your spouse has done to you during the past month. How could these occurrences have been prevented?
9. Recall a marital quarrel that took place in the recent past.

Did it end with bottled-up rage or resentment? Did it involve denigration of either participant? Review the quarrel in retrospect and discuss how it could have been handled more constructively so that it ended with an improved relationship instead of a bruised one.

10. Have there been occasions when you wanted to show affection to your mate and did not? What was the basis of your restraint? Give full details.

11. Name five pleasurable activities you've participated in together and five activities you've participated in alone in the past month. Which did you enjoy more? Explain.

12. Would you prefer more time alone? More time alone with your mate? More time in company? Explain.

13. What positive factors do you feel are missing from your marriage? Who do you think is more responsible for these voids; you or your spouse? Give your reasons for this conclusion. In addition, discuss each of the factors you feel are missing. For example, if you feel trust is lacking and you are more responsible for this, discuss the difficulty in this area.

14. Briefly describe three things that you have requested your spouse to do, correct, or improve, to which he or she has not been responsive.

15. Briefly describe three things that your spouse has requested you to do, correct, or improve but which you have not done.

16. Was there a period during your marital or premarital relationship when you would have been more accommodating to the requests described in question 15? If so, specify in detail the factors that account for your current unwillingness.

17. For each of the unfulfilled requests described in question 14 discuss the factors that, from your view, account for your mate's unwillingness or inability to please you.

18. Name five ways in which you'd like to change. Would these changes please your mate? Why haven't you implemented them?

19. Name five ways in which you'd like your mate to change.
20. If you have children, do they help or hinder your marriage? How so?
21. If you do not have children, do you want them? Why or why not?
22. Do you know of a couple whose marriage appears to be more fulfilling than yours? If so, what factors account for the strength of their marriage?
23. What are your aspirations and expectations for your marriage in the future? Be specific: for example, "I would like household tasks to be shared equally," "I would like my wife to become more affectionate," and so on. Name at least five aspirations. Describe what you are doing to insure that these hopes will be realized.

Children

Minimizing the Disruption

Parenting

Being a parent, as Sigmund Freud once remarked, is an impossible profession under even the best of circumstances; marital discord can escalate the difficulties to unbearable limits. When three generations of family members lived in the same house or nearby, it was easier to raise children. Grandmothers and aunts could counsel and help a mother who was distressed; a couple that needed time to themselves to work out their differences could ask another adult they trusted to take over for a while. Husband and wife could discuss their parenting problems with older and frequently wiser members of their family. And the children could find a loving adult with time to listen and to counsel—a sort of court of appeals. Today's parents share the responsibility for being everything to their children.

Childless couples can sometimes reconcile their marital differences and disappointments by ignoring the discords, pretending they do not exist. They can seek compensating gratifications elsewhere, perhaps in their work—it is simple for both of them to have jobs. However, when there is a child, this shift of emphasis is impossible, and the child becomes living evidence of the dissatisfaction in the marital relationship.

". . . We had been arguing for months. I was sure he was fooling around. I constantly accused him but he passed it off as a joke. When he did this, I pestered him about it even more, but he just ignored me or made more jokes. It nearly drove me nuts. I nagged him all the time. He finally began to get fed up with it and told me to fuck off; he even smacked me around a couple of times. But he didn't admit a thing: It was all childish and crazy but I couldn't help myself, and the more I bore down, the worse things got between us. All this wasn't doing Patrick anything but harm—he was nearly eight and he sensed the strain. He started bedwetting again and even stammering. His teacher said he was nervous in school. Maybe that woke me up—woke both of us up. Not only was our marriage troubled, but we were creating a toxic home life for our son. I decided to consult with a social worker acquaintance, and as a result my husband and I became convinced that we should all go into family therapy."

Games Nobody Wins

The presence of children in an unstable marriage does not mean that successful resolutions are out of reach, but it does complicate things, particularly if husbands and wives resort to misusing their children as weapons in the adult conflict. When infidelity results in (or contributes to) marital discord, some spouses not only blame each other explicitly for the failure in their relationship but implicitly involve their children.

For example, the wife may favor one child and the husband another; sometimes they bid for the same offspring and he or she may end up feeling like God's special gift to the world. A father up to his ears in debt who shells out for a new car for his teenage son, saying "I owe it to him," is probably involved in this ploy, as is the mother who wears her threadbare coat for another winter so that her daughter can buy that new dress she simply must have.

On the other hand, a child's life may be made extremely miserable because his parents are competing to find fault with him (the "fault" allegedly "inherited" from the other spouse). This strategy is a favorite way of getting at the partner who is more sensitive to the child's needs—which is one reason why it is dangerous in a distressed marriage for a child to be a favorite of one parent. This invites misuse of the child as a weapon. In extreme situations, it may even result in physical cruelties. In any case, the child is apt to suffer emotionally either through overindulgence of his whims or severe deprivation. The conclusion is likely to be the child's loss of respect for the parents and a perpetuation of infantile behavior. Moreover, the parents' conflicts, rather than diminishing, are likely to be increased.

Susan Carter is a high-level executive for a woman's-wear manufacturer. She travels a good deal and her husband resents both her success and her "freedom." As a strategy against his wife, Mr. Carter began to pamper their only child. He wanted to alienate the youngster from his mother in order to persuade her to give up her career and "stay closer to home."

> He: (disgusted) You're not doing your job. Jeremy is being neglected.
>
> She: (angry) You're crazy!
>
> He: (righteously) What do you mean, crazy? You're never around to take care of him. You're always running off.
>
> She: (insistent) Jeremy gets excellent care. Since when did you become father of the year?
>
> He: (accusing) How many nights have you been gone—doing who the hell knows what—and the baby woke up and I had to take him into our bed!

She: (counterattacking) What the hell are you taking a five-year-old into our bed for? Jeremy is well aware of my job and shouldn't ordinarily have any difficulty with it. Are you forgetting the times he has come to work with me and gone on trips with me? What about that? What about the time I spend with him explaining how I always come back? What are you trying to create?

He: (angry) I don't like it, goddamn it!

She: (accusing) That's it! It's you who has the problem. You resent me having an independent life. Your male ego's threatened!

Eventually Mr. Carter's destructive strategy succeeded to the point where Jeremy recoiled from his mother when she returned from her business trips. The Carters were divorced a year later.

Another common abuse of children occurs when they are used to undermine a mate's authority and power. A wife may do this by subtly or not so subtly encouraging or assisting the children to break the rules established by their father. For example, as the father backs down the driveway, he notices the children's toys in his path. He gets out of his car, throws the bicycles, baseball bats, trucks, and skates out of the way, dashes into the house, and shouts, "Goddamn it, Gail, have the kids keep the driveway clear. They have plenty of room to play all over the place. The driveway is off limits!" That night, returning from work, he hears the crunch of toys under the car wheels as he pulls into the driveway. He is fit to be tied. Storming into the house, he finds the family at the dinner table. Repeating the morning scene, he screams, "Who the hell left the toys in the driveway! How many times . . ." Gail, looking relaxed and unhurried, replies coyly, "John, it's probably my fault. I was on the phone with Joan

Edwards—you remember her, the one you found so attractive at the Smith's party last week—and I completely forgot about talking to the children." The husband turns, slams the door behind him, and closes the first act of "I'll Get You."

A related ploy for expressing hostility to a mate is "Victim-Villain." In one typical case, Mrs. Jackson returns from shopping late on a Saturday afternoon. Her children had been assigned to do the dishes in her absence. As she drives up to her home, she honks her horn, but nobody comes out to help with the groceries. Annoyed, she goes inside carrying one of the heavy shopping bags. There are dishes everywhere. The kitchen is a mess, nothing's been touched. Furious, she races upstairs, shuts off the blaring television, and angrily confronts her two children, aged ten and twelve. She yells, "What is the meaning of this? How could you be so inconsiderate?" At this moment, Mr. Jackson, who was reading his newspaper in the backyard, appears and is requested by his wife to intercede. In complying with his wife's request, Mr. Jackson allows his children to see that he is condescending to their mother. He implies "My heart isn't really in this, but I'd better say these things to get your mother off our backs." In admonishing the children, he manages to uphold his image as fellow victim and adds to his wife's image as villain. He is widening the gap between himself and his wife, and between his wife and the children—to the eventual disadvantage of all.

It might be emphasized that in both "I'll Get You" and "Victim-Villain," the issue is not parental disagreement about the children's behavior. Of course, important family decisions concerning children are best made jointly by mothers and fathers; an authentic united front makes excellent sense because it gives children clear-cut direction to follow or rebel against. On more trivial issues, parental agreement is not critical. Nevertheless, the behavior depicted above is the result of a hidden agenda, and to focus on parenting techniques would be to miss the point. The critical issue here is underlying hostility communicated to a mate through the children, to everyone's detriment. Jim and Martha O'Neill's fight about their children that turns out not to be about children at all may provide additional clarification:

> She: You're too soft on the kids. You can't just let them do whatever they want.
>
> He: I don't know what you're talking about. I simply told Bobby I'd rather he didn't go over to his friend's house. I didn't insist and he decided to go anyway—is that a crime?
>
> She: That's not the point. It's because you didn't insist that I have to take all the responsibility for the kids. Who disciplines them—me!
>
> He: I don't agree. I do my part. What the hell is bugging you?
>
> She: (angry) You're driving me crazy! I do all the dirty work. You prance through life without a care in the world. What is this? If you're not going to be home half the time, the least you can do is face up to your responsibilities when you're here.
>
> Therapist: Martha, it sounds as if you're angry because Jim is out so many evenings.
>
> She: (very red in the face) No, that's not it! It's just that he doesn't back me up when it comes to the kids—
>
> He: (interrupting) You're angry because the kids and I have such a good relationship. You're always trying to make me the "heavy."

She: Oh, bull!

He: Listen. I take enough responsibility just trying to earn a living. I think I deal with the kids just fine.

She: How do you know how well you deal with them? You're away so much of the time, you hardly see them.

Therapist: You know, Martha, Jim's being away so much really does seem to be bugging you. Is there something you want to say to him about that?

She: (becoming red in the face again) No. It's just that . . . . (beginning to cry) It's just that . . . .

He: . (uncomfortable, interrupting again) Come on, let's forget this, we're not getting anywhere.

The O'Neills thought they were battling about parental authority, "doing a good job of raising the kids," and the role of the "man of the house" but these proved to be superficial issues camouflaging more intimate ones that neither dared confront. It emerged that Martha suspected Jim was having an affair. Her suspicions arose because in recent months he was away from home more than usual, and when he returned, he did not make love to her as passionately as in the past. In later therapy sessions, Martha learned to level about her real feelings, wants, and expectations. The issue of disciplining the children never came up again.

Yet another tactic for wreaking psychological havoc is employed by the parent who makes pointed or allusive remarks about the unfaithful person's behavior in the presence of the children. This usually produces unbearable shame and guilt in the affair-involved parent—and is quite unsettling to the children. Often the accusation is delivered in the heat of battle—

"Don't give me that 'control yourself' crap! Why don't you control yourself with your girlfriend!" The rationalization here is "It's better to be honest with the chilren." But, of course, this type of fraudulent honesty is likely to put the children in the center of a game of "Charge and Countercharge." Also under the guise of being "open with the children" one parent is covertly pleading, "poor little me."

Margaret, a fourteen-year-old, describes her experience with this maneuver.

"My parents seem to be always fighting. They fight over the most ridiculous things. Sometimes, when they're both home, I go to a friend's house just to get some peace and quiet . . . . Last Saturday my father suggested we take a ride to the beach. Just me and him. When we got there, we walked around a little, then we sat and talked. He told me how my mother's always running around with other men and how she is immoral and all that stuff. He said he tries very hard to be a good husband and a good father but that my mother makes things hard. I was so embarrassed and uncomfortable. I didn't know what to say so I just sat there frozen. I didn't say anything to my mother, but a couple of days later, she started to talk to me and she said the same things about him! She said she tries to make us a decent home but my father is insecure and has to prove himself with all the young women. It was disgusting. I felt so alone."

Dr. George Bach in his valuable book, *The Intimate Enemy*, adds to and summarizes the roles children may play in the marital conflict:

Kids can be—and often are—used as:
1. Targets. This is most likely to happen when parents shift the brunt of their adult battles from spouse to child.
2. Mediators. As when the father says, "Tell Mommy to be nice to Daddy."
3. Spies. The mother says, "Go and find out what mood Daddy is in."

4. Messengers. The mother says, "Tell your daddy that I'd like to come back to him, but make sure he thinks it's your own idea."

5. District attorneys. The mother says, "I can't stand your father. But I'll stick with him because of you." Whereupon a child may say, "I'll help you get rid of him."

6. Translators. The child says, "Daddy didn't mean that. What he meant was . . . ."

7. Monitors. The child says, "Mummy didn't say that. What she said was . . . ."

8. Referees. The child says, "Why don't you let Mummy explain a little more? Let her talk."

9. Cupids. Parents, especially fathers, often cast their children as love releasers. The way to a man's heart my be through his stomach; the way to a women's heart is often through her child.

10. Audiences at adult fights.

Dr. Bach goes on to say that in times of marital discord, roles 1 through 5 are likely to be destructive, and others, particularly role 10, as we shall discuss later, may be either destructive or constructive.

Children's Games

As a refuge from their own emotional distress in an unstable family, children develop defensive games. Children's games, like their parents', spring from the need to survive emotionally. One such game is "That Will Teach You!" As in all manipulative strategies, the details of "That Will Teach You!" differ according to the methods of dealing with parents that children have found most effective—usually effectiveness is a direct consequence of the weaknesses of a particular parent. For example, a boy who knows his mother is proud of a clean house will continually leave his room in a state of chaos. A girl aware of her mother's concern for what the neighbors think will carry on a loud, revealing argument in public. A son will flaunt long hair and bare feet in his conservative father's face.

A rather dramatic example has been described by Joanne and Lew Koch in their book, *The Marriage Savers*. Psychiatrist Michael Soloman treated Ruth, a seven-year-old with symptoms of serious asthma. Dr. Soloman suspected that Ruth's asthma was related to family problems and decided to approach her condition by way of family therapy. Every time Dr. Soloman got close to some of the real problems in the family, the child would get sick and threaten to die. After he had worked with the family for nearly a year, focusing on the parents' relationship, Ruth said, "I think that I should be sick for the rest of my life." The mother said, "Why in the world would you say something like that?" This seven-year-old child answered, "I've figured out that when I'm sick, the two of you know what to do, and when I'm not, the two of you don't know what to do. If I'm sick, you don't fight. If I'm not sick, you fight." When Ruth's parents' relationship improved, so did her asthma. Dr. Soloman reports that Ruth had not been hospitalized or even seriously ill for three years following family therapy.

The "Divide-and-Conquer" routine is another favorite in distressed marriages. Seeking a gift, special privilege, a waived rule to provide reassurance, the child will play one partner against the other. "But Daddy (Mommy) said I could" is the opening line of this strategy. With a parent who is trying to enlist the child as an ally against his mate, this ploy is extremely effective. It works nearly every time. If the demand is too great and the parent refuses, a reminder that "Daddy said I could" or "I don't like you anymore; I'll go ask him, he's nicer" is usually enough to reverse the unfavorable decision.

When children consistently play destructive emotional games, it is often because their basic trust in their parents' ability to love and care for them has been undermined, and they believe they can only get the love and care they want through manipulation. Such children opt for attention even if it is negative. This yearning for attention that finds its expression in "impossible" behavior will diminish when parents provide a firmer feeling of love and security for the children.

Other Considerations

Behind many children's games is the unspoken plea, "I want you to know how I feel so that you will stop doing things that are making me so anxious and afraid. Show me that I am all right and that you love me." It is not always easy for parents to view matters in this light. It is much easier to accept obnoxious behavior as revenge for punishments, felt injustices, or other, unrelated developments. Usually these proclamations ("Jimmy's always been a nervous kid; it has nothing to do with us") are an avoidance of more heated issues. Sometimes, however, a child's emotional reactions are not directly related or are out of proportion to marital conflicts. With or without parental dissension, the process of growing up is stormy. Peer relations, school pressures, achievement aspirations, dating problems, all take a toll on children, and parents often become the toll collectors because they're convenient.

Some children (as well as adults) have inborn tendencies to emotional distress and acting-out behavior. This does not mean they are born with specific emotional and behavioral disturbances such as anxiety or violence, but they do seem to inherit tendencies toward irritability, introversion, or low frustration tolerance. Recent studies at the National Institute of Health show, for example, that from birth onward, children exhibit clear-cut temperamental differences. Long-term studies have demonstrated that the child who is inhibited at birth and in childhood continues to act in a similar fashion into adulthood, while the energetic, assertive child is more likely to become an energetic and assertive adult. Thus an inhibited youngster who is naturally very sensitive may feel that his mildly angry parents are very angry at each other; because of his overreaction, he may anxiously anticipate signs of another argument breaking out and again interpret the next mild conflict as a great hostile outburst, thereby creating more anxiety, feelings of insecurity, and so on.

This is not to dilute parental responsibility. The quality of the marital relationship and the manner in which conflicts are resolved certainly have an impact on children; however, they are not the only considerations. Children have their own problems, and their distress is not necessarily an indication that the marriage is faltering. It is a signal to examine the situation carefully for the contributing factors and an opportunity for parents to work as a team in providing for their youngster.

To Fight or Not to Fight

Childen frequently become upset by parental anger and fighting. Moreover, they often feel themselves to be the cause of parental conflict. This is particularly true of the chronically angry family. Given these realities, would it be best to spare the children this emotional burden by not allowing them to witness or be involved in marital discord? Many parents respond affirmatively and with some justification. First, there are times when the issues being discussed or argued are too sensitive and therefore inappropriate for young witnesses. Second, and more important, parents who tear each other apart in front of their children in scenes reminiscent of *Who's Afraid of Virginia Woolf?* are creating a very poor marital model for their offspring. These are tactics to be aware of and guarded against. The continuance of destructive interaction is an indication that professional intervention is warranted. Indeed, the recent trend to treat the entire family seeks the modification of these debilitating family battles as a primary goal. Without intervention, far too many children are likely to grow up thinking that marriage is an excessively troublesome and painful arrangement.

Considering the disadvantages, parents can decide not to argue in front of the children. The fact is, however, that simply not arguing in front of the children is a poor solution. Not only is it a virtual impossibility to have fights that the children won't become aware of, but a lack of open discussion actually robs the children of potential benefit. The one critical guideline is: Keep

the fighting aboveboard. Parental fighting in which both partners stay with the issues and do not resort to crude, manipulative strategies actually helps prepare children for their own
future marital fights and for survival in a very difficult world.

Marsha is a slim thirty-one-year-old woman with long black
hair and dark, searching eyes. She recently graduated from the
City College of New York and works part time as a laboratory
technologist. Marsha has been married for six years; she and her
husband Richard, who also works on a part-time basis, share the
rearing of their two children. Marsha describes her parents'
marriage:

" . . . They fought a lot of the time. You could hear them four
blocks away, but I think they were basically happy. I remember
many of their fights being followed by a resolution, a making up.
They said things to each other in anger that they apologized for.
They always made sure I was aware of the apologies. When they
got mad at me, I was told, 'Being angry doesn't mean I don't
love you.' When they were mad at each other, I was reminded of
the same thing—'We may disagree about some things and feel
very angry but that doesn't mean we hate each other.' They
taught me that a person may not like something about you but
still like *you*. This is a lesson that's made a critical difference in
my life. Rejection, for instance, isn't as traumatic to me as it is to
many people. I know, on an emotional level, that I can't be liked
by everyone. Rejection doesn't make me feel worthless. Another
thing, I think I am probably more assertive than most women.
Being wrong and possibly incurring somebody's wrath doesn't
frighten me. I've seen wrath and it's not so terrible."

Richard comments:

"I like Martha's folks very much, and I agree with her view of
their impact on her. I think she was very fortunate to grow up in
a household where people didn't believe in facades. Her parents
don't censor themselves and display only their best side. They
are very real. My parents, on the other hand, were petty, bickering, and indirectly hostile to each other. The display of emotion

was taboo. I picked up a lot of bad habits. First of all, I didn't speak up when something bothered me. I would sit and stew. When I did say something, it was aimed at provoking guilt in the other person; I tried to get my way by using emotional blackmail. The disparity between Marsha's style and mine made for quite a conflict. It's only in the last year or so that I have learned, mostly through Marsha's example, to speak up and say what I want and what's bothering me. No camouflaging. No beating around the bush.''

It may come down to this: To the extent that unexpressive or passive parents wean themselves from the notion that peace and quiet must reign, they will have moved to a starting position for conflict resolution. This is possible without undue harm to their children. In contrast, those partners who are chronically angry are probably banging away at the wrong issues and would best consider their posture in light of its potential damage to their children. Most important, fair fighting—that is, fighting in which both partners are honestly striving to resolve a conflict rather than to destroy an opponent—can comfortably take place in front of the children. Ideally, children will learn by example to fight for their wants and express their feelings constructively.

Naturally, some issues (e.g., extramarital sex) are best aired privately. Dirty, underhanded fighting is best done secretly. If this is the best level of fighting a couple can attain, they should consider professional assistance. A couple can tell if they fight poorly by the results—one or both partners are constantly hurt and conflicts are hardly ever resolved. Issues involving the children that are fought and refought but resist resolution despite compromise should be reconsidered. What if the children were not the issue—would another issue surface? If so, discuss it and see where it leads. Even under the best of circumstances, manipulative emotional games will be played, but as side events, not center-stage attractions. As parents become more aware of and are able to express their own feelings and their children's real needs, games of manipulation will yield to healthy and open communication.

Getting Out
Divorce and Separation

The Agonizing Showdown

Many men and women who desire extramarital relationships are not deterred by conscience but by practicality; they do not regard an affair as immoral, but as a serious violation of the marital code that could have harsh consequences including public exposure, marital strife, separation, and divorce. The urge to destroy the sexual wanderer sometimes becomes overwhelming. Formerly gentle spouses turn into seething monsters, lashing out and exposing family skeletons in order to "teach the son of a bitch a lesson." Even in an unhappy marriage, divorce is a grim prospect involving the breakup of the home and the division of property, the fierce struggle to win over the children, the disruption of friendships, and the harsh financial penalty that may be exacted of the adulterer.

The aggrieved spouse's lawyer is likely to make the road to divorce quite rocky, advising the affair-involved adversary to settle generously out of court since the judge is likely to be strongly biased against an adulterer. To the affair-involved husband, this often means unbearably high alimony payments and restricted opportunities to see his children; to the straying wife, little or no alimony and a custody battle.

The consequences of divorce are frequently hard on the punisher as well—financial ruin, embarrassment, and the breakup of the family. For a couple with children, divorce ends the marriage but not their mutual involvement, since the children are a link that neither remarriage nor absence can break. Rather than being a final settlement, the divorce becomes an adjustment the family has to adapt itself to, a process that may take several years.

Peggy Quinn is an attractive woman with style and grace. During the fifteen years she was married to Ed, she thought they had a good marriage. But now, four years after her divorce, she recalls that during the last five years of the marriage, she and her husband only slept together once or twice a month—usually after Ed had had a few drinks. Peggy accepted their deteriorating sex life as the inevitable consequence of many years together until one of her "kind" friends told her that Ed's pleasures and interests lay elsewhere. The weeks that followed were such agony for both that even before divorce proceedings were under way, Ed moved out. Peggy, suddenly swamped by the technicalities of living, felt lost. Not only did she have the responsibility for two children, food, and clothing, but for financial records and transactions that her husband had usually managed. In Peggy's words:

"The problems of starting over were unanticipated. It was extremely difficult returning to the job market after a ten-year absence, but it became necessary due to the increased expenses of a split household. I was unprepared for the attitude society had toward a divorced woman and how difficult it was to get credit. So-called friends dropped me socially. It was as if they thought it was not safe for me to be in the presence of their husbands. Do people think divorce is contagious? The loneliness was horrid, hours on the phone or sitting in front of the television were a poor substitute for a mate . . . . I had had most of the responsibility of child rearing and taking care of the house before the separation and divorce, but these tasks became much more tiring, meaningless, and thankless after working all day. I got very down sometimes thinking that now I was breadwinner, father as well as mother, housekeeper, laundress, *ad infinitum.* When my youngest developed medical problems, I had to take the major responsibility. Eventually she required surgery. At one point, I became almost suicidal under the pressure."

Children and money were the two binding agents that forced Peggy and Ed to continue seeing each other. These confrontations were very delicate and painful. When a man and woman have lived together for many years, the connective tissue— emotional attachment—does not dissolve so easily. A tone of voice, a gesture, a certain comment can twist a knife in either the rejector or the rejected. Peggy continues:

"The bitterness between Ed and me ran deep. The chill in each other's presence was devastating. It was several years before we were able to treat each other casually and lightly. For me, the process was filled with self-pity and hate. The thought that he had a lover waiting in the wings for the final decree drove me wild. When I thought of him with her, I became unsettled. All that we had worked for—he was making a good living; we had grown up together; I sacrificed, he sacrificed—now she, rather than I, savors the rewards of those difficult years. I couldn't accept the injustice! I was consumed with getting back. I thought of turning him in to the IRS for tax fraud. I considered blackmail, disfigurement, murder. I settled for giving him a hard time with the kids. I turned them against him by presenting an image of him as a bum; I made it hard for him to see them; I tortured him through them.

"Slowly, I calmed down and started to dream of a new life. This began about three years after the divorce. There were still hassles between us and awkward moments, but things were becoming reasonably civilized. I began to exercise, take care of my appearance; I started therapy, school, and dance lessons. It wasn't my intention to distract myself so as to lose the ache—by this time it was already muted—but to bring back the nerve. I was determined to face the world not as Peggy Quinn, amputated from Ed Quinn, but as a whole human being. I had run out of pity. Out of a long period of submergence in my marriage and the agonizing period of discontent followed by my continuing struggle, I am discovering something very important: me!"

Divorce need not be the signal that life is stopped and is never to be resumed. Peggy Quinn survived and eventually prospered. Many others—men, women, and children—have likewise succeeded in the face of broken marriages. Sadly, though, the process is typically characterized by animosity, revenge, retribution, and bitterness—especially if one of the spouses has a lover. Although such involvements are frequent, they are seldom the primary cause of divorce; rather they tend to be the catalyst in the destruction of an unsatisfactory marriage. This is difficult for some people to accept. To most of the Quinns' friends, the affair was held solely responsible for splitting up a "beautiful couple."

Today, almost everyone has heard of a marital split that seemed sudden and unexpected. Of course, this is rarely the case and a closer look at the Quinns' relationship reveals not fulfillment marred by a brief bout with lust, but a profound unhappiness resembling that of the characters in Elia Kazan's novel, *The Arrangement*. In this story, the protagonist has become increasingly dissatisfied with his marriage and at forty-three engages in a serious affair with a younger woman. He is confused by his behavior and feels guilty because he either doesn't understand or won't acknowledge that his wife's good nature is leaving him unfulfilled and conflicted. His wife, true to her helping nature, arranges a plan, a different "style of life" for the two of them, with the hope it will draw them together and rid her husband of his misery. The husband complies—out of passivity or sheer exhaustion—and for almost a year, they live in a way designed to protect the couple (him!) from the material and carnal desires that threaten their illusory togetherness. The arrangement, appropriately called the "fortress," backfires: instead of just eliminating the husband's lustful desires for other women, it causes him to become passive and impotent.

During the eleven-month fortress period, the husband and wife are the envy of all their friends. The wife's emphasis on the "pure" life and the husband's surface responsiveness project an image of sharing, togetherness, and unusual devotion. Below the surface, however, is serious conflict, for the dream of "happily ever after" is not shared; it belongs only to the wife. A near-fatal auto accident, which is recognized by the husband as a suicidal gesture, forcefully shatters the togetherness fantasy. The husband, after his recovery, leaves his wife.

Perhaps with less drama, but through an essentially similar process, Ed and Peggy Quinn's marriage dissolved. Although this couple appeared to share common goals, their "arrangement" was based on one person's dream. The other was silently off in a different direction. The affair that triggered the divorce was the fierce blow that knocked down the fortress.

There are occasions when divorce is more directly the result of an adulterous relationship. In these instances, it is the deceived mate's overreaction and the adulterous mate's guilt and defensiveness that bring the marriage to a halt. Thus what may have started as a casual episode for a person contented with his or her marriage but flattered by attention from the opposite sex is transformed into a divorce.

Friends may speed the movement toward divorce by taking sides and reinforcing the deceived mate's feelings of injustice and hurt, and the adulterer's sense of guilt. ("Haven't you hurt her/him enough already?") However gratifying it may be to receive the support of friends, it often does more harm than good. Yet the emotional damage one experiences after discovering a husband or wife is having an affair makes one crave this type of loyalty from friends. There is nothing sweeter than hearing a husband called a total louse for cheating on his lovely wife with some "call girl," or a wife denounced as an "ungrateful bitch" who doesn't deserve her hard-working husband. Such denunciations help to polarize the couple and interfere with their efforts to communicate and sensibly sort out their situation. This is not to say that discussion of sensitive issues with friends is best avoided. At times of crisis, friendship is especially valuable. However, caution is suggested in following the advice of a friend who may be too emotionally involved to be helpful.

False Alarms

Although divorce motivated primarily by adultery is rare, it is not uncommon for an individual to threaten divorce in an effort to keep a spouse in line. One wife who likes to show her husband that she is not to be taken for granted—and at the same time make sure that he is as fully committed to her as ever—stages a mock divorce ritual every few months by dramatically packing her bags, all the while screaming her complaints in a furious tirade. Each time as she starts phoning for a hotel reservation, her husband concedes. In this household, the false alarm serves as a jolting reminder to the husband that his wife feels strongly about his extramarital behavior and it works—temporarily. Too often partners who either threaten divorce or storm out of the house and isolate themselves in a hotel find that the payoff is disappointing:

"This was the second time I had discovered his infidelities. That was it! I told him he'd had it and I left. At first, I felt really great. I felt very much in control. I had a regal room in a luxury hotel. After all, I thought, if I'm going to leave, there's no use punishing myself. I might as well treat myself well. I ordered a dinner of prime ribs and a whiskey sour from room service and felt very much protected in this environment. In the morning, I ordered eggs Benedict, showered, and luxuriated in bed reading a copy of *Mademoiselle* I had sent up. I didn't feel angry at all; that had seeped out of me when I left my husband pleading with me to remain home.

"All this time I had not left my hotel room. The next afternoon, though, I decided to put on a nice outfit and go down for lunch. I sat at a little table in the hotel cafe and ordered a sand-wich and a drink. I didn't feel terribly comfortable sitting there myself. As a matter of fact, I was damned uncomfortable. In con-trast to my room, which felt safe, the place was large, austere, and impersonal. I imagined it as a refuge for the disconnected and lonely. I didn't like the idea of being part of this. After a while, a man approached my table and asked to join me. He looked decent enough and seemed simply to want conversation and company, but I got scared stiff and retreated to my room.

"That evening I really began to worry. I'd figured all along that I would go home again, but now I wondered if my husband had seen my leaving as final and whether he would be there when I arrived. Even if he was, would he be receptive? Would he make the first move? If he didn't, would I be able to? All these things began to trouble me, so I decided to call. I spoke to my teenage son and said, 'I just called to let you know that your father and I had a bad fight and I left. I wanted you to know where I am.' As I hoped, my son told my husband where I was, and he was at the hotel soon after with an apology. He promised to behave himself and we left for home together."

Certainly not everyone who temporarily leaves a mate suffers the high separation anxiety this woman experienced. Sometimes a respite from each other is a very useful experience for a couple: it offers an opportunity to function independently and to assess areas of overdependence; for some people, it provides a very im-portant "cooling off" or "time -out" period. The difficulty lies not so much in the separation but in how it is used. Often, rather than employing a brief separation constructively, a spouse is attempting to get back, to "teach the son of a bitch a lesson," and leaving then becomes a form of punishment. Predictably, after the punishment is administered, an emotional but super-ficial peace pact is drawn up. "You're right," one spouse may say to the other in a disarmingly nondefensive manner. "Forgive me, it won't happen again." At this point, the issue is likely to be neatly tucked away. The pattern is outburst; withdrawal; il-lusory resolution. It is as if both husband and wife silently consent to leave well enough alone. This pattern is most popular with compulsive gamblers, alcoholics, and emotionally troubled individuals married to "rescuers," and with couples who have a shaky marriage that one or both fear to break up. Unless the difficulties are discussed thoroughly and concrete compromises introduced, the pattern is likely to be repeated and become increasingly corrosive to the marriage.

To Divorce or Not

When is a marriage not working? When should one seek a divorce? An easily applied guideline to answer these questions does not exist because marriage is much too complex a process to fit specific formulas. Some general observations, however, may apply: A marriage is not working when you feel that you can function better without your spouse than with him. It is not working when you would rather be alone or with somebody else than with him—not sometimes but usually. It is not working when you think your children would profit from the absence of your spouse. A marriage is not working when there is no fun in it. When, then, should a couple wisely consider divorce? In most cases, not without professional consultation. Then, whenever it is clear that husband and wife are not functioning together without severe damage to one or both, physically or emotionally, and that the destructiveness is irreversible or reversible only with an effort that is not forthcoming from both partners.

Once it is determined that a marriage is not working and is unsalvageable, divorce is the best way to assure the sanity of the partners and, especially, of the children. Youngsters are infinitely better off with divorced parents than in a subtly crazy-making family. Unfortunately, many couples caught in an irreversible and mutually destructive process do not get out. They persist, despite the lack of emotional closeness, and the consequent psychosomatic illnesses, infidelities, disturbances in their children, and general misery. Here are some of the reasons for the deadlock:

1. The one who would like to initiate the divorce feels that doing so would be an admission that he or she is wrong and that the other is right after all. Or if one decides to leave, the "deserted" partner may try to prevent the separation in order to avoid the suggestion that he, having been abandoned, is inferior and the spouse who left is superior. These couples remain together not out of love but out of hate. As one woman put it, "I'd leave the philandering bastard in a flash, but I'll be damned if I am going to give him the opportunity to come out of this thing a wounded hero!"

2. Each partner may want the other to assume the responsibility and guilt for the breakup. For example, neither may want to play "bad guy" or "home wrecker" in front of the children, so they stick together in order not to let the other have this advantage. Little thought is given to what such an arrangement does to the children.

3. One or both may be excessively afraid of loneliness. Most people abhor loneliness; some are terrorized to the point where being left alone makes them feel like an abandoned orphan. They marry to avoid being alone—or to be "rescued" from their parents—and once married, they cannot tolerate being alone for more than a few hours. This is like having a fear of the dark—except that it operates around the clock. Both usually end up more lonely than before they were married. And to the loneliness is added bitterness. For each is fragile and requires constant reassurance from the other. If this is denied, the "rejected" spouse draws back and the other now feels rejected. The distance between the two quickly increases. Usually these people find it difficult to be intimate with anyone, although out of need for reassurance, they act passionate and may have had a number of affairs. They continue together, quietly destroying each other, because of a fear of being apart and alone. They do not want to face what faces them.

Aside from the psychological reasons for avoiding a divorce, there are practical factors that couples offer for continuing the relationship. Primary among these is financial circumstances. For middle-income families, the expense of two households (not to mention legal fees) presents a formidable barrier to divorce. The financial hardship, and the psychological needs discussed above, should be weighed against a living arrangement that slowly eats away at integrity and well-being.

Lovers United?

If a marriage is broken by an affair and the lovers do not marry, the extramarital involvement is likely to be seen as an irresponsible fling. In contrast, marriage of the lovers seems to provide justification for the divorce. It is then assumed that the original marriage was unhappy and that the illicit transgression was sincere and honorable. The affair becomes sanctified by marriage, and the couple can once again enter society's fold. This is the idealized version. In actual life, it is a rarity.

Morton Hunt in his study *The Affair* states that of the unfaithful people he interviewed, only about one out of ten had married, or were about to marry, the person with whom they were having an extramarital affair. Regarding those interviewees in his study who were affair-involved and divorced, Hunt explains, "Only part of these divorces were sought in order to marry the partner outside; even when they were, the planned remarriages took place only about half the time."

There are many reasons why the majority of lovers do not marry after a divorce frees them to do so. For one thing, an affair resembles courtship and divorce alters this. During the affair, lovers limit themselves to a narrow behavioral and social repertoire aimed at pleasing each other. Often this repertoire consists of precisely the kind of behavior lacking at home. In addition, there is the excitement of "lovers against the world"—the clandestine adventure includes secret trips, sojourns at hotels under false names, and so on. Their emotional investment in these risks convinces the lovers that the affair is the high point of their lives. With the divorce, the drama calms down, and while the strains of secrecy and jealousy are removed, new ones are introduced. For example, a lover may "cop out" after being exposed to some unfamiliar and unpalatable divorce-battle behavior—his depleted finances, her ugly emotional outbursts, vindictiveness—all of which have a dampening effect on romance. Now the lovers really get to know each other and some of the revelations may be totally unexpected if not shocking.

The experience of Jeffrey Fisher provides an illustration of a downhill slide. Mr. Fisher, after separating from his wife, moved in with his mistress. For the first time in their two-year relationship, they were able to assume the roles of man and wife. Soon conflict appeared. Jeffrey was passionately involved in his profession. Helen demanded he be more attentive now that they were finally together. In the past, she had understood his difficulty in seeing her—he was married. Now, she insisted, there was no excuse. If he worked late, she became upset. If he was tied up in his job for several days in a row, she was irritated, resentful, and openly antagonistic. Jeffrey, seeing this side of Helen, began to have serious misgivings about marriage, although he had felt certain for months that he wanted to marry her. Helen, sensing the withdrawal, felt frightened and betrayed. As a result, she became more antagonistic and on many mornings provoked an argument just before Jeffrey departed for the office. Jeffrey then began to work even later, and Helen felt more left out than ever. The cycle lasted six weeks; the new marriage, conceived in idealism, died unborn.

Sometimes children complicate the picture. One man, childless, came to know his lover's children for the first time after she obtained a quick Mexican divorce. Not used to children, he became easily annoyed with them, particularly since they were demanding a great deal of attention during this difficult and confusing period. He constantly snapped at them, which only made them more demanding of attention. Their mother was in the middle. At times, she sided with him and agreed that "the children needed discipline," while on other occasions she demanded he be more tolerant of their behavior. Though she felt compelled to try to keep the children in line ("If they don't behave, he'll leave"), she hated herself for being cruel to them. Her former husband began to appear increasingly desirable, but he would have no part of her. Finally, after four months, her lover left. He walked out without explanation; there was none needed.

These are some common complications that can destroy lovers' desire to marry, but even under more harmonious circumstances, an extramarital relationship can falter after divorce. A harsh divorce fight hardly promotes enthusiasm for another marriage, so many new divorces suddenly find themselves reluctant to take the plunge again.

"I met him at a party given by my publisher at the close of summer two years ago. We spent the fall and winter getting to know each other, a time which I will cherish as the most unambiguously wonderful of my life. After a long, exciting winter, we decided we wanted to try living together. He was single. I was involved in a marriage of convenience. There were no children. I left my husband despite his promise of a bitter, contested divorce battle and moved in with Eric.

"I found living with Eric sort of comforable. It was much better than living with my husband. But I had a nagging sense of uneasiness. Once I was free, I was jumpy about getting tied down again. Eric wanted very much to get married when the divorce came through but I didn't want that. I was feeling tied down with him. For instance, he expected me to be with him for dinner every evening and that bothered me. I don't want always to be occupied with the same person. I hadn't really explored standing on my own two feet—or other men. First there was my husband—we were married very young—then there was Eric. I wanted to chase around or be chased around a little bit. . . . I felt so pressured to make the right decision that at one point I thought of committing suicide. My fantasy of suicide, it turned out, constituted the bottom line for me. Conflict that had been burrowing within since adolescence regarding independence/dependence, masked quite marvelously by the sacred bonds of marriage, was now out in the open. The choice became to face life by myself or spend the rest of my days angry. I decided not to commit myself to Eric. We split up and only see each other occasionally now."

When an affair that contributes to the breakup of a marriage by its promise of a fresh start fails to evolve into a new marriage, is anything to be gleaned from the experience? Yes and no. Some people, particularly the pathologically insecure, the compulsively promiscuous, the highly guarded and defensive who disallow intimacy in their lives, learn little. For them, extramarital involvement, whether it contributes to discord and eventual divorce or drones on undiscovered, is an empty experience, except perhaps for some physical joy. They bring little to a love affair and receive little from it. For others, however, the dissolution of the affair is not all pain and loss. Conversations held some time after the expiration of both the marriage and the competing affair attest to this. From Jeffrey Fisher:

"My marriage was a disaster. It was a relationship that can only be described as consistently destructive. Unfortunately, my relationship with Helen began to be tainted with the same rigid, destructive elements that had existed in my marriage. This time, though, I was aware of what was occurring and I put a stop to it before it got out of hand. Helen and I are still friends. We didn't allow our differences to destroy us but we would never have made it together. Work is my passion and I realize that very few women are going to be willing to become a distant number two in my life. I complained viciously to my wife and to Helen that it was unfair of them not to accept my priorities. But it was equally unfair of me to demand that they change their wants and goals. Nobody was at fault. As a matter of fact, realizing this, I am on better terms with my wife and women in general than ever before. I may just be one of those people not well suited to the type of commitment marriage requires. One of these days that might change, but if not, I think I can live a reasonably satisfactory life without marriage."

And this from the woman seeking independence:

"I've learned a number of things on my own. More often than not, the learning of them has been a lonely business, but I suspect I might have been unable to grasp the point of things in any other way. I have a renewed confidence in my personal effectiveness. From daddy to husband to lover was just too much. I lived with the fear of being left empty and, more simply, of being left. It was a horrible state. I had lost the ability to think, to imagine, to feel. Being completely on my own was the only way I could claw my way back to independence. Emotionally, I am stronger for the experience. My relationship with men has an adult-relating-to-adult quality rather than the parent-child pattern I experienced in the past. I've served a much needed apprenticeship with myself. One of these days I might even try marriage again. I think I am almost ready to handle it on more mature terms. This little girl has become a woman."

But what of the extraneous sexual involvements that do evolve into a marriage? Morton Hunt asks in his study, "Do they confirm the romantic myth that lovers who have struggled long to possess each other live happily ever after, or do they belie it?" He concludes:

> They do both. Although the available evidence is scanty, it would appear that about half work out well, while about half fail—a failure rate little higher than that of second marriages in general. Still, one might consider this rate high in view of the depth of involvement and the long period of testing that preceded the marriage. . . .
>
> Perhaps, then, there is something about the illicit origin of such marriages that dooms them: The puritan conscience would find such an answer intellectually and morally satisfying. Indeed, in a fair number of cases, there does seem to be a special kind of marital problem or cluster of problems that relates to the way the relationship began. But when one looks more closely, it seems clear that for these difficulties to prove hurtful, there must have been pre-existing psychological pa-

thology in one or both persons, or in their relationship to each other.

Hunt goes on to describe factors such as guilt toward the rejected marital partner, which is directed toward the present mate; disturbed relations with the opposite sex, which, undetected during the affair, are expressed in the marriage; and the loss of the excitement that the clandestine nature of the affair had provided.

Lovers united? Sometimes yes and happily. Sometimes not— or yes, but unhappily. Influenced by passion, consumed by hope, giddy with love (or revenge), the recently divorced, whether "rejected" or "rejector," would better stop, think, and *wait*. Going from one marriage immediately into another, even if preceded by a long-term adulterous relationship, is dangerous. At a time of emotional weariness from the divorce process, the individual is least likely to exercise sound judgment. Living alone for a time, or experimenting with trial cohabitation, improves the odds for success the second time around.

The Coping Process

There are no typical divorced people but there are emotional reactions and adjustments that are common to most divorced people. First, there are the problems of living alone. The divorced woman frequently must learn how to handle money, particularly if her husband (and before that, her father) has managed the finances. Her long-time social and economic dependence will leave her feeling bereft. She may panic, not occasionally, but frequently. Usually, she has the children, which present at once a burden and an incentive to conquer the pain.

For the man—who frequently also has long-standing habits of dependence—the children and the comforts of home his wife provided may be sorely missed. Rights of visitation seldom compensate for daily contact with the children. Learning to cook, create a comfortable living environment, and cope directly with laundries, supermarkets, and the endless details of daily living may appear overwhelming. Rather than bother, some men resign themselves to hotels or furnished rooms that only make their lives bleaker.

Husband and wife share a complex and confusing interplay of emotions: anger, sadness, guilt, fear, relief, excitement. The final decree is a release from the bickering, delays, recriminations, legalities, and lawyers, but sometimes the release is short-lived. A sense of failure and doubt may prevail: "Is there something wrong with me, some fatal flaw that propelled me into this circumstance? Is there someone out there with whom I will be able to form a close relationship? Am I capable of that?"

From the initial separation through (and often after), the divorce, an emotional digestion process occurs. During this time, a number of attitudes and negative emotions may burst in and out of daily experience—anger, jealousy, plots of revenge, loneliness, and panic. After a reasonable period of time, which may range from several weeks to perhaps a year, the divorce is likely to be digested. Sometimes it is not. When separated or divorced partners fail to wean themselves from each other and continue to experience intense guilt, fear, dependence, and hate, they go through life like battle casualties. They may congratulate themselves on their freedom, but psychologically they resemble zombies. Below are some of the more common emotional and attitudinal traps that occur during and after the separation and divorce process. They are natural reactions, yet if they continue to be intense and frequent long after the divorce has been finalized, they will be serious inhibitors.

1. *Stereotypic thinking.* "No man can be trusted" or "All women want is your money" or "Men are only out for sex." These statements serve as protective shields. What people who make these statements are really saying is, "I have been hurt and I am scared of being hurt again; since men (women) are no good anyway, I have ample reason for avoiding them." It is this attitude, not the basic "evilness" of men or women, that prevents the divorced individual from going out and meeting new people.

If an individual does socialize but continues to see people through rigid preconceptions, a self-fulfilling prophecy is likely to occur. That is, if people are treated with suspicion and mistrust, they are likely to return in kind, confirming the divorced individual in his opinion that most people have something up their sleeve, are deceptive, can't be trusted, etc.

2. *Blaming.* Blame is corrosive. It eats away at life, blighting the capacity for joy and intimacy. The woman who keeps calling her ex-husband an s.o.b., the husband who keeps telling his new wife or lover what a witch his former wife was, are bound to taint their new relationships. Rather than remaining judgmental and belittling the ex-mate, it is more productive to ask, "Now that I am single, what have I learned from my past marriage about myself and what can I do now to make my life more satisfying?"

3. *Self-pity.* Next to blame, which can be turned inward in the form of depression or outward in the form of anger, self-pity is the most damaging emotional reaction. Most unhappy divorcés are too embroiled in self-pity to live in the present or plan for the future. They repeat and reinforce former destructive patterns, see themselves as helpless victims, suffer from a succession of ailments and fatigue. The more energy and time they put into self-pity, the less they have available for building a new life.

4. *Unrealistic expectations.* Some people have very unrealistic expectations of how other people should be. They demand a perfect world with perfect human beings, and become angry, frustrated, or withdrawn when things don't go their way. Since reality hardly ever measures up to their superstandards, they have a good excuse for not attempting any new undertaking or socializing. Since they anticipate a negative, disappointing consequence before they start, a start is never initiated. The failure here is to accept that we live in an imperfect world and that all the people in it are also imperfect. Disappointments are necessary for growth, change, and development. If a person is not willing to accept the fallibility of other human beings and life's in-

evitable frustrations, his chances for fulfillment are small indeed.

5. *Fatalism.* The fifth and final barrier is the mythical belief that most human unhappiness is caused by other people and outside events and that a person has virtually no control over his own destiny. Blaming, stereotypic thinking, self-pity, and other similar behaviors are all symptomatic of this self-avoidant view; these are ways we avoid responsibility for our own self-created misery.

In contrast to the "I am a victim of my circumstances" philosophy is one that expresses self-responsibility: "I have the capacity to change and find greater fulfillment." In most areas of human interaction, there are few things that cannot be accomplished. If you think "I can't face my employer and request a raise; I can't lose weight; I can't get back into the social scene," ask yourself the following questions: If someone pointed a gun at your head and threatened to kill you if you didn't do what you say you can't do, would you do it? If your child or some other person very dear to you was in life-threatening danger and their only salvation lay in your doing what you say you can't do, would you do it? If the answer to either of these questions is yes, then ask yourself, "How is it that I won't do things for my own happiness?"

These, then, are some of the factors that impede successful living during and after a divorce: stereotypic thinking, blaming, self-pity, unrealistic expectations, and fatalism. Support and sustained help from friends who not only offer a shoulder to cry on but also the reassurance that they wholly accept and value you can help the reconstructive process. Time is also important—wounds close slowly. Meaningful activities, social service, politics, college classes, and various self-improvement regimens also prove helpful for many people. Most critical is a hard and painful effort directed toward altering self-defeating attitudes. For this, professional assistance or a local self-help divorce group may be beneficial.

How do you know when the wounds of the separation and divorce process are healing properly? Mel Krantzler in his sensitive book, *Creative Divorce*, offers some guidelines:

Resentment and animosity toward your former mate have diminished in intensity, duration and frequency.

You become more concerned with solving problems than complaining about them.

You call up old friends and begin making new friends, convinced that you have nothing to be ashamed of.

You begin making decisions based on your interests and pleasure—taking a course, attending a play, entertaining friends.

You no longer view the opposite sex in general as threatening or despicable, and statements lumping all men or women together no longer seem accurate to you.

You become aware that you are not the only person who has ever been divorced, that other unhappily married people have had the courage to do the same.

You accept your divorce as the only possible solution to a self-destructive marriage and not as a punishment for having failed.

Seeking Professional Help

Better and Worse

Barbara and Mark were married for twelve years and had two sons. During the last year, Barbara had been involved with another man. She didn't know whether to leave her husband or to break up the affair and try to work on improving their marriage. She suggested they both go for marital therapy. Mark was bitter and complained that therapy would be a waste of money: "I'm not crazy. You'd better straighten yourself out or leave. I'm staying in this house; I'm not leaving my children just because you've had a change of heart." Barbara wasn't about to give up her home or children. She continued her plea for a third party until Mark reluctantly agreed to give therapy a try. Barbara and Mark give a summary account of their experience; Mark comments first:

"At the time Barbara suggested therapy, I was enraged. I'm a decent guy. I try to do the right thing. This is what I get in return? I thought, 'Goddamn it, I don't deserve this!' Besides being angry as hell, I was embarrassed. Going to a stranger and telling him that when I roll over toward my wife in bed I feel her tense up isn't my ideal way to spend an evening! On top of all this, I felt I was living out a prophecy. My father died when I was very young, and my mother remarried and divorced twice. I've always had the nagging suspicion that having grown up in a broken home, I was destined to end up in the same circumstance. This angered me also. I felt I never stood a chance. I was also angered about the possibility of losing my children. As a child, I knew what it was to lose a parent. I didn't want what happened to me to be repeated with my children. All in all, I was one angry guy. And all my anger was pent up. Once in a while, I would blow off at Barbara but usually I carried it around. I was like a bomb ready to explode. For the first time in my life, the thought of suicide occurred to me.

"During that first session, I was beside myself. I had this feeling of inevitability. I felt Barbara was going to leave and that nothing would stop her. I felt the way people must feel when they're about to be executed. I felt helpless and empty. I remember that when the therapist mentioned that he understood I was in pain, I practically jumped on him. 'Psychologist or not,' I yelled, 'you can't know what I'm going through unless it happened to you!' He wasn't defensive about that. He said, 'You're right. I can't experience your pain, but I sense it; I also hear it and I want you to know that.' He said that in a way that told me he really meant it. I believed him, and it relieved me because I didn't feel I had to work at convincing him how bad I felt. I began to cry."

Barbara:

"My choice was either to leave or to find a way of satisfying myself within the marriage. I knew I was driving Mark up the wall. He was starting to drink too much and he wasn't sleeping well at all. He was doing everything to contain himself. I married when I was eighteen—straight out of high school. My father was very strict, and I saw Mark as an escape. Probably lots of people have done the same. Now I was going through a reevaluation. I really didn't see why I wasn't happy in my marriage. Why couldn't I get as much from Mark as I got from this other guy? I knew the only way I was going to work this out was with a therapist.

"One of the early things the therapist said to us was, 'I'm not in the marriage-saving business. I don't regard marriage as sacred. I regard personal happiness as primary. If the two of you can learn to contribute to each other's happiness, that's terrific. If you detract and you are either unwilling or unable to correct this, then it's up to you to decide where to go from there.' I felt a little taken back by his statement. He seemed to be implying we would have to make a lot of our own decisions about things. I guess I was expecting him to tell us what to do. I had secretly hoped he would give me 'permission' to leave. I remember asking him what he thought about me leaving. He wouldn't say, 'Yes, go,' or 'No, stay.' Instead, he helped me look at the consequences of staying and leaving. It was still up to me. I knew that in the final analysis, I would have to decide, but I was aching for someone to take me off the hook."

Mark:

"During the first few sessions, I had to deal with my anger. Barbara is very even-tempered. I am angered easily. This was the case even before our difficulties. In therapy, I was encouraged to be more expressive and this felt good. I began to say a lot of things to Barbara that I hadn't said before. But things between us got worse. I said to the therapist, 'You suggested I communicate more, really express what I'm feeling, and when I do express what I'm feeling, what do I get back? Shit!' I was getting just what I got as a child. When I opened my mouth, I got a slap. The therapist encouraged me—us—not to give up. He reminded us that pain is not a signal to run."

Barbara:

"After five months of therapy, we began to see some real changes in our relationship. The biggest thing that happened was we began to appreciate each other as individuals—adult individuals. We had been so busy catering to our view of each other's weaknesses, so preoccupied with taking care of the other person, that we were both suffocating. It was a tremendous relief not to have to take care of the other but to trust in his ability to stand on his own. This was liberating for both of us. In therapy, we both began to appreciate—if not always liking—each other's honest thoughts and feelings. We didn't feel we had to be overly careful about hurting each other or causing one of us to fall apart. We began to believe in each other's strength."

Mark:

"Finally after several more months, we made a joint decision to terminate therapy. We wanted to do things on our own. It's not that all our problems went away. There wasn't anything magical like that. We just began to feel more like struggling with them without any extra help. I guess we had come to a point where we felt we understood and appreciated each other. We felt we could live our lives and be fulfilled even without each other. Also, for the first time in years, we were genuinely cooperative and positive with each other. We learned to compromise to our mutual benefit. Our relationship took a mature turn. We became more desirous of each other and truly enjoyed each other's company."

In this successful marital therapy experience, Mark and Barbara were helped in several ways, some of which may not be evident from their brief description. They were assisted to: develop clear communication so that the message sent is the message received; identify the behavioral patterns and attitudes that were deteriorating their relationship; take responsibility for their part of the marital disruption rather than blame the other; practice techniques designed to increase cooperative and positive behavioral patterns and decrease negative, relationship-defeating behavioral patterns; develop the ability to negotiate and create workable compromises. These are the critical areas of intervention. To the extent that a breakdown occurs in one or more of these areas, marital distress is likely to increase. A couple seeking assistance from a competent marital therapist can expect help in each of these areas.

Unfortunately, as another couple, Carl and Virginia, were to learn, therapy can also be a negative experience. Unless therapy is approached skillfully, the dissatisfactions and destructive patterns in marriage may be escalated rather than diminished.

"We had been having difficulty in our marriage for some years. We really didn't have a partnership. Virginia had the kids to mind, no job, few friends. I was busy all day in a demanding job, trying to rise through the ranks. I would come home after being gone for nine or ten hours and just drop in front of the tube. We lived in separate worlds. Virginia always felt that I was too dominant and that she had to subjugate her personality to mine. She was probably right. . . . Then there was the sexual problem. We were married at eighteen, and in the beginning of our marriage, I was very unsure of myself sexually. I lacked experience. I was uptight about performing. I had a very strict Catholic upbringing; my Catholic schoolteachers and my parents seemed very down on sex—'This is a thing you don't do.' I remember the first time I masturbated, when I was about fifteen, in confession, I was chastised. Psychologically, it was pretty effective. I felt guilty as hell for a year after that if I so much as thought about masturbating.

"Virginia is the one who called Jack for an appointment. He was recommended by a friend. We were both pretty taken aback by Jack's manner and appearance in that first session. He was a big man, with a very large bald head, and he was sitting in the middle of his living-room office in a yogalike position. He was very informal and almost insisted we call him by his first name immediately. During that initial session, he encouraged us to accuse each other. I thought that one of the sanest things we had going was that we weren't into pointing to each other and complaining 'You're to blame.' Jack said that wasn't how we really felt. 'What you really need,' he insisted, 'is to go through an emotional upheaval.' He made the point that I especially needed this because I was the one creating the problem.

"In our second session, Jack said he had been thinking about our prior discussion and he had come up with a possible solution. 'I'm not going to tell you how to run your life.' he started, 'but I think you both need a broader sexual experience. Have this within your marriage,' he continued. 'Maintain your marriage and have coexisting outside relationships. This will test your commitment to each other. If you are really for each other, you can share this experience and it will strengthen the relationship.'

"My first reaction to Jack's statement was shock—and fear. He picked up on this and convinced me I needed this experience if I was ever going to relate satisfactorily to a woman. He said this experience would provide a definition of the real me. I would find myself. Virginia needed less convincing. She admitted that she had some curiosity about outside sexual experiences, which, I thought, was only natural since her experiences with me were not satisfactory. So we listened to Jack and agreed that maybe he was right about the open-marriage thing. That ended our second session.

"It turned out that the guy who recommended Jack—my friend—was the guy Virginia wound up in bed with. She told me about it one night in intimate detail just as Jack had suggested —'share the experience.' I was devastated. I don't remember ever being so uncomfortable. God, it was a painful experience. Now I was ready for blaming! But who could I blame? I had agreed to this insanity. For the first time in my life, I became impotent. It was two months before, out of sheer desperation, I called Jack for another appointment. This time just for me—to discuss the impotence. He was very casual about it. He asked how long I had been impotent. I told him for over two months. His reply was, 'Don't sweat it, you'll get over it. It's natural for these things to occur.' He started telling me about his own experience with impotence but I interrupted him. His casual, offhand 'hey, just lean back and enjoy the trip' manner was no consolation. I felt psychologically and sexually powerless. I left the office before the end of the session. I didn't pay him or even say anything. I just got up and walked out. That was the last I saw of him. I never heard from him again. The next day I moved out of the house and took a small apartment. The divorce came through three months later.''

There are several points to be made regarding Carl and Virginia's brief "therapy" experience: It is important in a prior telephone call or initial session to obtain information regarding the therapist's credentials and point of view. Beware of the therapist who imposes personal biases (e.g., pushes open sexual involvement). This does not mean that therapists are not to have personal beliefs or that they are not to be expressed; only that they be honestly labeled as biases and not imposed. The therapist who views his role consistently as a judicial one in which he sifts the evidence presented and eventually makes pronouncements is, at best, inexperienced. This approach tends to be extremely damaging because the spouses involved are likely to devote their energy and ingenuity to digging up "evidence" against each other. The result is an escalation of bad feelings and an increased schism until the therapy—and the marriage— break down altogether. Therapists who side with one or the other spouse on an overall basis ("You're the problem"), rather than as a temporary therapeutic maneuver or on a particular issue, are destructively reinforcing the false idea that at the heart of marital problems is a victim or a villain. This behavior sometimes occurs when under the pressure of gender liberation, therapists lean over backwards to side with the spouse of the op- posite sex in order to "prove" fairness. The view that a couple should accuse each other and blame the marital disturbance on each other is decidedly counterproductive. Bitter quarreling over pointless issues, particularly if it goes on session after session and is encouraged by the therapist, is not an indication of an "intense emotional upheaval" but of an incompetent therapist for allowing the destructive behavior to continue.

Danger Signals

How does a couple know if marital therapy is warranted? Marital distress may range from overt anger to underground dissatisfaction taking the form of avoidance. The most obvious "red flags" indicating that a couple should consider getting the assistance of a professional third party are these:

1. Frequent arguments without resolution in which one or both partners are left with hurt feelings or burning resentment. Special emphasis would wisely be placed on those very sensitive issues involving the suspicion or discovery of an affair. Sometimes the conflict takes the form of consistent arguments over what appear to be insignificant issues. Constant arguments about the children are frequently a clue that the children are being used as a "buffer" between marital partners.
2. Feelings of being ignored or unwanted by the family ("I'm only useful as a money maker (maid), otherwise no one really gives a damn").
3. Frequent avoidance of each other. There are numerous ways people living together can avoid each other. Sometimes a couple manages to have other people around all the time—frequent house guests, friends for dinner, friends to share vacations, friends to spend weekends with—hardly ever giving themselves an opportunity to be alone. These are usually the couples whose divorce amazes their friends who thought they were "wonderfully happy together." The television set is another convenient barrier. Overwork or overinvolvement in avocational pursuits can also be a danger signal.
4. Overdependence on the part of one or both partners. This

can be expressed by constant "checking" on each other, not feeling comfortable and worthwhile without a mate's companionship, resentment of a mate's independent interests, living for a spouse's achievements, and being overly sensitive to a spouse's criticism.

5. Sexual dissatisfaction. This includes lack of attraction, inability to "let go" in bed, a lack of affection, warmth, and mutual sexual pleasuring. Also significant are compulsive extramarital sexual relationships, particularly those in which deficiency motives such as hostility and revenge are primary.

These are some of the more common danger signals; there are an infinite number of variations. When should you seek help? Not after a short-lived, shallow dip in domestic satisfaction. A day's arguing over the children, a few days of melancholy or self-pity, a siege of jealousy—these are not necessarily signals of trouble. They are more probably results of the normal strain of living in a difficult world. The key to watch for is repetition—a *continued* feeling of resentment, boredom, lovelessness, hurt, and sexual dissatisfaction.

What Not to Expect

When we are little children and we fall, bruising our knee, Mommy or Daddy kisses the injury and makes it all better. They do magic. When we get sick and the doctor comes, administers some pills, and cures our ailment, the doctor does magic. When we are grownup and have marital problems, we go to another type of doctor, the marriage doctor, expecting that he or she will make the marriage all better—like magic. Unfortunately, therapy doesn't work that way. There are no magic pills, no magic wands to wave. *A passive stance—"Therapy will make us all better"—is an unrealistic attitude that guarantees therapeutic failure.* This is probably the most common unrealistic expectation that couples bring to therapy, and it is probably similar to the erroneous attitude that the marital relationship will prosper by itself—"Now that we're married, the relationship will grow." Most of us are aware of the falsity of the latter notion, but it is a tempting trap. In actuality, a marriage works because the husband and wife work at it. This applies equally to therapy.

Other expectations that increase the likelihood of dissatisfaction with therapy are these:

1. *Marital therapy is a process designed to keep the marriage together.* This is *not* true. Therapy is supposed to help couples clarify their own needs, wishes, and feelings and to identify in their spouses those traits that meet their needs and those that do not. The attitude of a professional is likely to be: My job is to help these people stay together more compatibly and productively or to help them separate as amiably as possible. Since this is not my marriage, it is not within my province to decide which of these two courses to take.

2. *The marital therapist, being an intelligent individual, will see my side of things and straighten my spouse out—"He (she) is really the problem."* Very often this is the hidden agenda. One mate seeks a collaborative relationship with the therapist in order to straighten the "sick one" out. If the therapist acquiesces, the therapy may seem to be going well for the "righteous mate" but the marriage is unlikely to improve. More likely, it will deteriorate. A more productive attitude involves shared responsibility for dissatisfaction with the marital relationship.

3. *I should feel comfortable throughout therapy.* It is not comfortable to change old habits, and since change is a primary goal, the therapeutic process is likely to be painful at times. Unruffled feelings are an unreasonable expectation considering that sensitive issues are being brought to awareness and confronted as never before. Also, the progress of the partners is likely to be uneven so that when one opens up, the other may rebuff him or her. Result: hurt and angry feelings. A sensitive therapist will support the rebuffed

partner, encouraging that partner not to give up while helping the other to be more responsive. But still it hurts. Discomfort in therapy is unavoidable; the absence of any discomfort is a sign that the process is merely superficial.

4. *If we are sincere and work hard, things will improve immediately.* Change is not easy and it is not instant. A relationship may even worsen before it gets better. Dissatisfaction, hurt feelings, anger, and misunderstanding are not quickly cleared up. Yet there is a tendency, after a few sessions, to conclude things are all better. Frequently, this is a premature decision based on an avoidance of further exploration of "hot" issues.

5. *We can always go into therapy in the future; things aren't that bad now.* One of the biggest exasperations of marital therapists is that couples hesitate to seek help until the situation is desperate. Then, in deep disturbance, they come to the therapist and expect to be bailed out. By this time, the relationship may have been severely damaged and the willingness of husband and wife to work at it almost exhausted. Little can be done to help marriages that are extremely disturbed. They generally break up in the end, and the partners unfairly ridicule the skills of the therapist when, in fact, a Solomon couldn't have prevented the breakup. If these same couples had begun therapy earlier, before things became intolerable and all caring stopped, they could have been spared years of marital suffering and misery.

Types of Marital Therapists

There are three major classes of mental health practitioners—
—psychiatrists, psychologists, and social workers. There are also professionally trained marriage counselors who offer treatment services to the public. Since it is important to know something

about the several classes of marital therapists in order to make a more informed choice, a brief discussion of each follows.

PSYCHIATRISTS

All psychiatrists are physicians who have completed medical training and have obtained a medical degree (M.D.). In some states, a psychiatrist need not have completed specialized training beyond the medical degree to practice psychiatry. That is, a physician with no special training in human behavior can call himself a psychiatrist or marital therapist with no approval necessary from a public accrediting body. Rather than formal training in the psychology of marital problems or supervised experience in helping persons solve their most pressing problems through psychological means, the physician without advanced training has been primarily schooled in handling patients administratively with drugs and hospitalization and giving rudimentary psychological first aid.

Psychiatrists who have had advanced training, particularly those who have completed the requirements of the American Board of Psychiatry, have usually spent approximately three years in psychiatric residence beyond the four years in medical school and a general (medical) internship. A good part of the residency may have been at a large mental institution such as a city or state hospital. In this setting, the people with whom the psychiatrist dealt were likely to be severely disturbed, such as schizophrenics or chronic alcoholics. Some time of the training period, usually about six months, is spent working with neurological problems (disorders caused by pathological abnormalities of the brain or nerves) and some time is frequently devoted to work in an outpatient clinic, where the physician sees a variety of patients with a variety of problems.

Some psychiatrists doing psychotherapy and marital therapy rely too heavily on medical methods, especially the administration of psychoactive drugs (e.g., tranquilizers). This is certainly not the rule, but it is most common among those with insufficient advanced training in individual and marital therapy. Lacking the proper experience to intervene effectively with individuals and couples seeking to resolve the (nonmedical) problems of living, the insufficiently trained psychiatrist is likely to prescribe tranquilizers in an effort to give his anxious patient something. Unfortunately, problems of living are rarely solved by tranquilizers. Drugs may temporarily ease anxiety, but if effective therapy is not pursued, self-defeating patterns are unlikely to be reversed.

Ascertaining the psychiatrist's methods of practice may be accomplished in several ways. Asking someone who has seen him in therapy may be helpful. The psychiatrist may briefly discuss his orientation in a telephone conversation. If nothing is known about the psychiatrist except that he is qualified—that he has an M.D. and has completed the requirements for the American Board of Psychiatry—an initial consultation is wise. The couple should arrange to meet the therapist together and jointly ask about his methods and point of view. Asking pointed questions of the therapist as to his training, experience, and attitudes may seem rude or unnecessary, but it should be remembered that therapy is an important and usually expensive venture whose success depends, in large part, upon the choice of the proper therapist. Couples may have to visit two or three different psychiatrists before finding an individual with whom they both feel comfortable and confident.

To see if a psychiatrist is actually board-certified, consult a volume called *The Directory of Medical Specialists* at a local library or medical school. Or write:

> The American Board of Psychiatry and Neurology
> 1603 Orrington Avenue
> Evanston, Illinois 60201

The American Board of Psychiatry and Neurology does not make referrals. These can be obtained through a local medical association.

PSYCHOLOGISTS

A professional psychologist is an individual who has a doctoral degree from a regionally accredited university or professional school in a program that is primarily psychological in content. The doctor's degree takes four or five years beyond the four-year college degree to complete. This includes a one-year supervised internship. All states have laws regulating the practices of psychologists. In the case of psychological practice that involves service for a fee (such as marital therapy), appropriate registration, certification, or licensing is required. Most states forbid anyone not so registered, certified, or licensed to represent to the public any title or description of services for a fee incorporating the words, "psychology," "psychological," or "psychologist." In addition to state laws, which usually require the doctorate and licensing by exam, to be listed in the National Register of Health Serivce Providers in Psychology (available in most public libraries), a psychologist must have two years of supervised experience in health services of which at least one year is postdoctoral and one year is in an organized health service training program. Because a psychologist does not have a medical degree (in psychology the doctorate is the Ph.D., Ed.D., or Psy.D.), he is not allowed to administer drugs or other forms of physical treatment, such as insulin or electric shock. If chemotherapy is deemed necessary, the psychologist will refer the patient to a medical doctor for a prescription.

All psychologists are concerned with the dynamics of personality and behavior but their training varies considerably. Although as a group psychologists have far more extensive training in principles of human behavior than the general run of psychiatrists or social workers, they may not have had specialized training in applying their knowledge to individual or marital disturbances. Some have a strong background in experimental psychology, which includes testing theories of behavior on lower animals. Others focus on industrial psychology or personnel management—fields that have little relevance to marriage counseling. Psychologists in the private (or agency) practice of individual and marital therapy usually have a background in the more therapy-relevant specialties of clinical or counseling psychology, but it is wise to ask the practitioner about his or her specific experience. The National Register of Health Service Providers in Psychology mentioned above lists the names of approximately nine thousand psychologists who have applied and met the licensure and experience requirements for inclusion. Psychologists are listed alphabetically and geographically by city and state. If this valuable resource is not available in your local library, referral information may be obtained by writing:

> The Council for the National Register of Health
> Service Providers in Psychology
> 1200 Seventeenth Street, N.W., Suite 403
> Washington, D.C. 20036
> Tel. (202) 833-7568

Since listing in the Register is voluntary, some psychologists, though qualified, will not be listed. Additional referral information can be obtained through a county or state psychological association.

SOCIAL WORKERS

The minimum standard for a professional social worker is a master's degree in social work (M.S.W.) earned by the completion of a rigorous two-year program of graduate study in an accredited school of social work. In addition to receiving the required classroom instruction, candidates for the degree work two or three days a week in an agency that offers counseling services, such as a psychiatric clinic, a hospital, a probation department, a welfare department, or a family counseling clinic. This internship, spread over two years, is supervised by an experienced social worker who holds the M.S.W. degree. Usually, individuals accepted into a graduate school of social work have an undergraduate degree (B.S. or B.A.) in one of the social or behavioral sciences.

Thirteen states have laws which license or certify the practice of social work and there is national certification by the Academy of Social Work as well as strong local, state, and national (National Academy of Social Work) organizations that strive to enforce professional standards. Most social agencies are sensitive to professional standards and in only a few, such as departments of county welfare, is the term "social worker" used for individuals who do not have the M.S.W. degree. A couple desiring marital therapy would normally not be applying for this service at a welfare agency, but at a family counseling service where the professional degree is required for employment. In seeking a private practitioner, an inquiry as to whether the individual has earned the master's degree in social work from an accredited institution is warranted.

It is important to ask the social worker questions regarding his or her professional experience. One pertinent question may be, "Have you had supervised experience in marital therapy?" Typically, social work students are offered a general program during their two years of training. This includes group work, individual casework, and community organization. A few social work schools provide for specialization in one of these areas. Thus, a student interested in training in marital and family therapy may be assigned a family counseling agency for internship. Others may obtain specialized training after obtaining the graduate degree. Although social workers are frequently given less status by the public and by other professionals, with appropriate training, they are as qualified to do marital therapy as psychiatrists and psychologists trained in this area. It is not so much the professional title as the individual's training, experience, and personal qualities that determine a successful therapy relationship.

To check qualifications or find a nationally certified social worker, write:

National Association of Social Workers
1425 H. Street, NW
Suite 600
Washington, D.C. 20005
Tel: (202) 628-6800

MARRIAGE COUNSELORS

"Marriage counselor" is a general term that can include social workers, psychologists, psychiatrists, pastoral counselors, and individuals with a master's or doctorate degree in psychology, family relations, educational psychology, guidance counseling, or religion. Many of these counselors have received neither theoretical instruction nor practical supervised experience related to marital problems. Some, however, such as those majoring in family relations or marriage counseling, have received excellent training. Perhaps an important factor in allowing those with inadequate clinical background to practice is that in most states the title "marriage counselor" is unregulated. As of 1977, six states had specific regulations concerning marriage counseling. They are California, Michigan, New Jersey, Utah, Georgia, and Nevada. Although anyone can practice in this field in those states where there are no regulations, there is a national organization for accrediting and certifying practitioners:

The American Association of Marriage & Family Counselors
225 Yale Avenue
Claremont, California 91711
Tel: (714) 621-4749

Membership in this organization of several thousand is strictly voluntary, but the qualifications for accreditation are rigorous. To become a member, a counselor must have a graduate degree in one of the behavioral sciences plus at least two years of clinical experience in marriage counseling under supervision approved by the Association. A couple contacting the AAMFC will be supplied with a list of three (or more) accredited counselors in their geographic area.

The Search

Finding a satisfactory therapist is often difficult. Sometimes recommendations made by friends, physicians, and lawyers are useful; other times they are not (a therapist who is quite helpful to one couple may not be helpful at all to another). Public reputation is often a clue, but sometimes the popular therapist is the one who pleases rather than effectively intervenes. Some marital therapists without academic credentials are very talented. However, in a field where incompetence and fraud are not uncommon, it is safer to choose a therapist who has had reputable training and experience. Unfortunately, professional qualifications do not indicate whether a therapist has had minimal, uninspired, or top-quality preparation. Further, since all forms of therapy are a mixture of art and science, the personality of the therapist is also important. A marital therapist may be a happily married man or woman who accepts life, marriage, and people, or a dour individual whose marriage is sterile and who approaches marital problems with a "what can you expect" attitude.

Sometimes marital therapists are very directive in their approach, to the point of becoming impatient or irritated if their clients fail to follow their suggestions immediately; sometimes they are so timidly nondirective that their clients feel they are providing the therapist with an interesting hour of conversation and gaining nothing in return. Occasionally a practitioner will have a moralistic attitude toward sex, divorce, or life itself that is conveyed in judgmental proclamations about "right and wrong." Or, the therapist may have an irresponsible, "liberated," egotistical attitude that causes confusion and uncertainty. Even the best therapist with the best training is bound to have bad days and is certain to do better with some couples than with others. And however well intentioned, a therapist's interventions cannot always be correct. The mark of a professional is not perfection; it is a willingness to admit mistakes and learn from them.

It should be clear by now that you must be cautious in choosing a marital therapist. Obviously, these warnings can be used to provide justification for those who wish to avoid therapy or who want to quit because the going is rough. This is not the spirit in which the cautions have been offered. Competent professional intervention has improved many ailing marriages; effective therapists have helped couples to reconsider their relationship and move in more constructive directions; this type of exploration is not being discouraged. The point is that to increase your chances of reaping the very real benefits of therapy, you should be able to evaluate a therapist with some sophistication.

Whenever we go to a doctor, a lawyer—anybody in authority —the child in us is apt to come out. We don't question; we don't trust our own judgment. But in making a decision about a therapist, one's own judgment is critical. After credentials, personal qualities, and reputation have been considered, the final decision as to compatibility rests on the couple's shoulders. The most effective way of making this important decision is to get referrals from several sources, including professional associations, friends, and other professionals, and to shop around. Admittedly, this procedure can be expensive because a few visits to a therapist may be necessary before a reasonable judgment can be made, but it is also possible that the first therapist chosen will prove to be quite suitable. To aid in making a realistic appraisal of the therapist, a list of seventeen questions adapted from Lazarus and Fay's book, *I Can If I Want To* follows. Responses are scored from 0 to 4; 0 equals never or not at all; 1 slightly or occasionally; 2 sometimes or moderately; 3 a great deal or most of the time; and 4 markedly or all of the time. Circle the number that best reflects your feelings and observations and then obtain a total score.

1. I feel comfortable with the therapist.   0   1   2   3   4
2. The therapist seems comfortable with me. 0   1   2   3   4
3. The therapist is casual and informal
   rather than stiff and informal.   0   1   2   3   4
4. The therapist does not treat me as if I
   am sick, defective, and about to fall
   apart.   0   1   2   3   4
5. The therapist is flexible and open to new
   ideas rather than pursuing a point of
   view.   0   1   2   3   4

6. The therapist has a good sense of humor
and a pleasant disposition.   0 1 2 3 4

7. The therapist is willing to tell me how
he/she feels about me.   0 1 2 3 4

8. The therapist admits limitations and
does not pretend to know things he/she
does not know.   0 1 2 3 4

9. The therapist is very willing to
acknowledge being wrong and
apologizes for making errors or for being
inconsiderate, instead of justifying this
kind of behavior.   0 1 2 3 4

10. The therapist answers direct questions
rather than simply asking me what I
think.   0 1 2 3 4

11. The therapist reveals things about
herself/himself either spontaneously
or in response to my inquiries (but
not by bragging and talking incessantly
and irrelevantly).   0 1 2 3 4

12. The therapist encourages the feeling that
I am as good as he/she is.   0 1 2 3 4

13. The therapist acts as if he/she is my
consultant rather than the manager
of my life.   0 1 2 3 4

14. The therapist encourages differences of
opinion rather than telling me that I am
resisting if I disagree with him/her.   0 1 2 3 4

15. The therapist is interested in seeing
people who share my life (or at least is
willing to do so); this would include
the significant people in my environment.   0 1 2 3 4

16. The things the therapist says make sense
to me.   0 1 2 3 4

17. In general, my contacts with the
therapist lead to my feeling more hopeful
and having higher self-esteem.   0 1 2 3 4

Drs. Lazarus and Fay suggest they would not be comfortable working with a therapist rated below fifty and would strongly advise against one whose score fell below forty.

In marital therapy, it is important that the therapist chosen be rated favorably by both partners because a big difference in regard is likely to add to an already strain-burdened relationship. As mentioned earlier, it sometimes takes several sessions before a reasonable judgment can be made. Other times, couple-therapist compatibility will be less ambiguous and a much quicker decision will be rendered.

Cost and Length of Therapy

One of the most important considerations for many couples is the cost of therapy. The range of professional fees is very broad. The majority of therapists charge between $25 and $60 per session for their services. A session may last from thirty to sixty minutes. Community agencies and family institutes, both public and private, generally have lower fee schedules and may even have a sliding scale based on income. Listings of these agencies are available in the reference section of a public library or through a local mental health association. Here are several suggestions regarding fees:

1. It is wise not to become involved with a therapist whose fees you will not be able to afford on a weekly basis for at least several months.
2. When there is legitimate financial reason, it is not "impolite" to ask if a therapist will reduce the fee. Some will, others won't. Most won't offer unless asked.
3. Do not regard size of fee as a reflection of ability. There is no relationship. Some competent therapists have a relatively low fee schedule, others bordering on incompetence are exorbitant.
4. Whatever the fee, it is not unusual to feel resentful. Payment for an intangible service is hard to accept. Most

payments result in something that can be driven, eaten, worn, or shown off. Therapy provides none of these.

Just as fee schedules vary, so do recommendations concerning the frequency with which a couple need to see the therapist and the length of time the therapy takes. In many instances, it will be suggested that therapy occur once a week jointly. Sometimes it is suggested that in addition one or both partners be seen individually. If the marital difficulties are quite serious, therapy is likely to continue for one or two years. It may be on a weekly basis, but more likely, as progress is made, the frequency will be decreased. Sometimes, although the problems appear severe at first glance, progress is established in a relatively short time and methods for continuing progress without therapy are suggested. Regardless of the duration of therapy, it is doubtful that progress will proceed in a neat forward direction. Rather, periods of stagnation, or even backsliding, are to be expected. Freud termed these reverses "negative therapeutic reactions" and ascribed them to an unconscious sense of guilt that barred improvement. While there is good reason to believe that Freud's explanation is ill-suited to the dynamics of many people, periods of "two steps back" and stagnation are part of even the most successful therapy experiences.

Epilogue

The material for this book came from intensive interviews with well over one hundred people. Their demographics—age, sex, religious and educational background, geographic location, socioecomonic status—varied but they are reasonably representative of the American middle class. As stated at the outset, this book is not a formal scientific study yielding definitive data. However, just as statistical studies provide valuable information, the experiences and feelings of individuals explored in depth contribute to our psychological understanding.

Why one becomes unfaithful, the conditions under which affairs are most and least likely to be troublesome, and how to cope with the effects on one's marriage are complex issues. Nonetheless, these tales of the affair-involved have suggested some guidelines. Here are the highlights:

To be or not to be sexually faithful is for most married people a perplexing decision. Nearly everyone feels the temptation to be unfaithful in married life. These extramarital yearnings may be confined to fantasy or mild flirtation, or the desire may be realized in a sexual encounter. The affair, like marriage, ranges from low to high in emotional involvement and neutral to grave in consequences.

The affair may be a cry for help, a struggle to attain health, or the acting out of an inner disturbance. There are many kinds of marriages and many kinds of adultery; all monogamy is not blissful and healthy and all adultery is not painful and sick.

When adultery occurs, some marriages gain, others lose; some mates grow, others deteriorate. Sometimes the effects of an affair are temporary and of no real consequence; other times they have critical impact and are long lasting. That adultery must adversely affect a marriage or that it is always a symptom of a troubled psyche is a myth; it is not having an affair in itself that counts but the state of the marriage (some are so unstable that they might eventually crumble even without the push of an affair); the motivation of the adulterer (e.g., if he seeks to hurt his spouse he probably will); the attitude of the noninvolved spouse toward himself (particularly is this critical if the affair is discovered); and the meaning the affair has for the marital partners.

Extramarital involvement often complicates a marital relationship. Again, the conflict may range from almost nonexistent to severe. If there are children, some of the manipulative emotional games adults in conflict play will probably involve them. If the adults usually fight fairly, the children are less likely to be harmed. However, if underhanded, dirty fighting is common, children will probably be used as pawns and suffer.

When an affair, either open or undiscovered, is symptomatic of a poorly functioning relationship, the marital partners may decide to repair and reconstruct their relationship. Reversing the negative trend in a marriage is difficult. Both partners will need patience, courage, and a desire to change. It is important that the couple learn to express their wants, preferences, and feelings unambiguously. Empathy, sharing responsibility for the marital difficulties, and a willingness to compromise are also key ingredients.

When self-help does not progress or is rejected by one partner continuously, aside from remaining with the status quo, divorce or professional intervention are possible alternatives. Divorce is a grim option. It is costly and emotionally wearing on the whole family. Most often divorce is the result of a deteriorated marriage rather than an extramarital relationship. Splitting up is sometimes warranted but it is highly advisable to seek professional help before making a final decision. The sooner professional help is sought the better. A careful and informed choice of a competent, compassionate therapist, along with a basic understanding of the therapy process, will provide the best chance of a successful resolution.

Is there one grand conclusion to be drawn from all this? Hardly. There is, however, a trend to report: Practically all of us desire a lasting relationship that is satisfying. We have a great capacity—or at least a potential—for intimacy. Yet this is not easy to develop nor, sometimes, is it easy to find another person with whom we can have a relationship of mutual growth. Mutual growth is at times as painful and difficult as it is joyful and rewarding. But when both partners are trying—where there is respect for the identity, equality, and integrity of the other— obstacles such as extramarital affairs can be successfully worked out.

It is worth the effort. In a period of rapid and sometimes chaotic social change, human relationships, especially a long- term and intimate one such as marriage, offer something of value worth hanging onto. Even with its limitations, marriage is, for many of us, one of the best and most enduring means of fulfill- ment.

Bibliography

Bach, George R., and Wyden, Peter. *The Intimate Enemy: How to Fight Fair in Love and Marriage.* New York: William Morrow & Co., 1969.

Bell, Robert R., and Peltz, Dorthyann. "Extramarital sex among Women." *Medical Aspects of Human Sexuality* 8, March 1974, p. 10.

Broderick, Carlton B. "Should a Husband or Wife Confess Infidelity? *Medical Aspects of Human Sexuality* 5 (1970): pp. 8–15.

Hunt, Morton. *Sexual Behavior in the 1970's.* Chicago: Playboy Press, 1974.

Hunt, Morton. *The Affair.* New York: New American Library, 1971.

Jong, Erica. *Fear of Flying.* New York: Holt, Rinehart & Winston, 1973.

Kinsey, Alfred C.; Pomeroy, Wardell B.; Martin, Clyde E.; and Gebhard, Paul H. *Sexual Behavior in the Human Female.* Philadelphia: W. B. Saunders Co. 1948.

Kinsey, Alfred C.; Pomeroy, Wardell B.; and Martin, Clyde E. *Sexual Behavior in the Human Male.* Philadelphia: W. B. Saunders Co. 1948.

Koch, Joanne, and Koch, Lew. *The Marriage Savers.* New York: Coward, McCann & Geoghegan, Inc., 1976.

Krantzler, Mel. *Creative Divorce.* New York: M. Evans and Co., 1973.

Lazarus, Arnold, and Fay, Allen. *I Can if I Want to.* New York: William Morrow & Co., 1975.

Llewellyn, Charles E. "Should a Husband or Wife Confess Infidelity?" *Medical Aspects of Human Sexuality* 5 (1970): 14—15.

Meyers, Lonny, and Leggitt, Hunter. "A New View of Adultery." *Sexual Behavior* 2 (1970): 52—62.

Neubeck, Gerhard (ed.) *Extramarital Relations.* Englewood Cliffs, N.J.: Prentice-Hall, 1969.

Pike, James A. *You and the New Morality.* New York: Harper & Row, 1967.

Rimmer, Robert. *The Harrad Experiment.* Los Angeles: Sherbourne Press, 1966.

Stone, Abraham. "The Case Against Marital Infidelity." *Readers Digest* (May 1954), pp. 11—14.

Spotnitz, Hyman, and Freeman, Lucy. *The Wandering Husband.* Englewood Cliffs, N.J.: Prentice-Hall, 1964.

Watzlawick, Paul; Weakland, John; and Fisch, Richard. *Change.* New York: Norton, 1974.

Whitehurst, Robert N. "Extramarital Sex: Alienation or Extension of Normal Behavior?" In *Extramarital Relations,* edited by G. Neubeck, pp. 129—145. Englewood Cliffs, N.J.: Prentice-Hall, 1969.

Winn, Harold. "Should a Husband or Wife Confess Infidelity?" *Medical Aspects of Human Sexuality* 5 (1970): 8.

Index